XA

MAKING EARLY STRINGED INSTRUMENTS

The author

MAKING EARLY STRINGED INSTRUMENTS

Ronald Zachary Taylor

STOBART DAVIES LTD

By the same author
Make and Play a Lute

British Library Cataloguing in Publication Data

Taylor, Ronald Zachary, *1936–*
    Making early stringed instruments.
    I. Title
784.1923

ISBN 0–85442–051–7

Published October 1991 by

STOBART DAVIES LTD.
Publishers & Booksellers
STOBART HOUSE, PONTYCLERC
PENYBANC RD, AMMANFORD SA18 3HP
Tel: 01269 593100 Fax: 01269 596116
www.stobartdavies.com

se, Priory Street, Hertford, Herts SG14 1RN

Typeset in Palatino by Ann Buchan (Typesetters), Shepperton
Printed in Great Britain by BPCC Wheatons, Exeter

DEDICATION

To Ramon Casal,
Professor of Lutherie at The Universidad Popular de Vigo

We have shared troubles and triumphs.
We have shared wine, food, and a workbench.
We have created music, instruments and a great friendship.

Un abrazo fuerte de tu amigo,

Zachary Taylor

CONTENTS

LIST OF ILLUSTRATIONS

LIST OF PLANS & DETAILS

INTRODUCTION

The purpose of this book is to provide information in sufficient detail to permit the making of a variety of musical instruments. My publisher was inspired to commission it after seeing the drawings I had prepared and used for my own reference in my endeavours to produce accurate copies of known originals. In most cases these were early stringed instruments which have been used by the Rozata Consort of Ancient Music which I am privileged to direct.

My intention, therefore, is to present a selection of instruments based on originals, suitable for playing in groups. The possibilities for teachers of craft subjects is obvious and it should be mentioned with emphasis that no previous experience of instrument making is necessary to produce the designs contained in this book. Nor is a knowledge of music needed, in either the practical or theoretical sense.

Since more or less standard tools are required, plus a few desirable devices which may be readily produced from details given herein, there is no reason why these authentic musical instruments should not be made by the average keen woodworker.

Even those less familiar with the skills of reading drawings are catered for in a section giving some guidance to their interpretation.

I hope that in some measure this book may assist, inform or inspire others who, like myself, enjoy making the magic of music a personal and exhilarating experience.

"For we are the music makers. We are the dreamers of dreams."
ARTHUR WILLIAM EDGAR O'SHAUGHNESSY 1844–1881

Ronald Zachary Taylor 1991

1. Historical Comment

My research into the background of the instruments featured in this book covers about twenty-five years of devoted study. It includes a working knowledge, to performance standard in some cases, of the music associated with them, together with a genuine appreciation of the people who made and played them. My studies took me to humble chapels and lofty cathedrals, into places forgotten by the present "pot noodle" culture, and never heard of by lager-louts. Places where music means a link with the most precious and sacred events that shaped our past, and not simply a noisy vehicle to promote the sale of potatoes processed in some unusual fashion. Do not misunderstand this opening, I am no moralist, nor am I a preacher or Saint. Nor am I scholar enough to call myself a "mediaevalist", worse luck. I am a man of my time with an appreciation of the music of yester year, some feeling for the instruments it was played on and an affinity for the people who made them.

I am sure that it was not possible to isolate music and instruments from the vast jig-saw puzzle which makes up the complete picture of this subject. Nor was it possible to indulge in an appraisal of the past without comparing such things as moral attitudes and cultural values. I must also say that standing at the threshold of the nineteen nineties, the more I contemplate tomorrow, the more I prefer yesterday.

Lest I be accused of being morbid, which I am not, or pessimistic, nor am I that, let me present a brief historical appreciation of the musical instruments in this book, and to conjure enthusiasm for this fascinating and living gateway to the past. . .

". . . when music, heavenly maid, was young"   W. COLLINS 1721–59

The Bowed Psaltery

This most accessible of all the instruments herein, was plucked before it ever had a bow laid across its strings, and whilst it works beautifully when plucked with a plectrum, or quill, the sound produced with a bow is sublime. There is an ethereal quality in its crystal tone that hangs as if frozen in the air. Little wonder how many times it is referred to in passages from the Bible, as in Samuel I, Chapter 10:

". . . thou shalt meet a company of prophets coming
down from the high place with a psaltery. . ."

Chaucer also knew the psaltery and was clearly smitten by its magic as in The Miller's Tale:

"And all above there lay a gay psaltery
    on which he made on nights melodie,
So sweetly, that all the chamber rang
    And 'Angelus ad virginem' he sang"

It appears in many forms, including the shape of a pig's head (strumento di porco), an angel's wing, and varieties of the triangular shape of our example, in illustrations readily referred to, from the 12th to the 15th centuries.

Figure 1   The Bowed Psaltery

Rote or Lyre

This is a most ancient instrument and is one of the easiest to play. Illustrations of the lyre being played by King David, who was said to have invented instruments, are almost too numerous to mention. There are also some surviving relics which afford us some excellent technical references, as in the 7th century example found in the ship

Figure 2   The Rote or Lyre

burial at Sutton Hoo. The one chosen as our model is from one excavated from a 6th century soldier's grave in the Black Forest. Obviously, with so few strings the melodic possibilities are restricted, although it is possible to "stop" the strings to increase the range but this requires much careful, and knowledgeable, practice. It was said to be used to accompany the recitation of rhymes and catches as an aide memoire, hence the phrase "to learn by rote". I have no proof of this, but see no reason to question it, either.

Some of our very early illustrations of instruments are those of the rote, or lyre, most of which are of the typical quadrangular shape made up of a soundbox, two arms and a cross-bar carrying tuning keys. One familiar shape of a lyre which is also used to symbolize music is that made of two curved animal horns attached to a tortoise-shell, and very elegant, too, in its somewhat primitive way. This basic shape may be seen decorating various parts of other instruments, as well as a feature of several classic pieces of furniture.

Compostelan Lute

I feel responsible for the naming of this lute "Compostelan", a term which in fact simply distinguishes it from a very large family group. A pair of these small instruments are part of the archway of the Santiago Cathedral.

In July 1989 I was one of five luthiers privileged to address an international conference on the subject of the re-construction of the instruments of El Portico de la Gloria. This was held in Santiago de Compostela and directed by one of the great musicologists of our time, Jose Lopez-Calo, who created, by careful selection, a group of people who became a fraternity almost overnight. My subject was the lute which is featured in this book.

In presenting the possible origins of this appealing little instrument, I looked at all of the elements which went to make it what it is, and compared these with all that I could find from my research. It would be very easy to use the time-worn and common-place reference to the Arabic influence on, not only the lute, but on many other Spanish instruments. (And their architecture, their art, their music and other aspects of their culture. . .) However, just to describe the instrument physically brought it into comparison with instruments of a much earlier epoch, and from a different country, Egypt. Very similar lutes have been found buried, painted on walls or otherwise depicted answering so similar a description as to make a whole study of its possible link with Egypt of paramount importance to instrument development in the West.

Figure 3   Compostelan Lute

Appalachian Dulcimer

Genealogically speaking, this is of the zither family and not a dulcimer at all, but it may be traced to multifarious origins by different names from all over Europe and covering several centuries. Compare the *Epinette des Vosges*, the *Langeleik, La Vielle Fille* and the *Scheitholt*, et al.

It is a homespun affair although this need not mean crudely constructed, as reference to some makers from the mountainous area from which its name is derived will quickly verify. The dulcimer is treated with serious study both as an artistic vehicle by maker and musician alike.

The nature of the dulcimer is to provide a "white-note" scale, that is, "diatonic". This limits the performer to few keys, in fact, depending on the tuning of the drone strings, it must be regarded as a "modal" instrument. This is not the place for me to indulge in a small thesis about the modal system, intriguing though it may be, but those who may as yet be unacquainted with it should find an excursion into its mysteries rewarding and applicable to this, and other, instruments.

The various ways of playing the dulcimer include plucking the strings with the fingers, or strumming with a plectrum, even bowing with a violin bow. The left hand stops the strings either with the fingers or with a small stick called, rather quaintly, a "noter".

The instrument appears in a wide range of shapes and sizes as its Arcadian origins might lead one to suppose, but generally there is a preponderance towards the elongated hour-glass shape reminiscent of a slender guitar.

It is a great buskers' instrument and enormously entertaining to play and to listen to, if in the hands of a good player.

Figure 4   Appalachian Dulcimer

Flat-backed Mandolin

In its mode of playing and viewed from the front it is virtually indistinguishable from the traditional Neapolitan mandolin which has a rounded back similar to the Renaissance lute. In fact, were it to have six pairs of strings (which the Genoese and Milanese versions have) rather than its usual four pairs, it would be a candidate for acceptance into the cittern family.

The flat-backed mandolins are much more readily produced by the amateur maker than are the types with round backs, and although they make a different sound from their rotund cousins it is incorrect to regard them as musically inferior. Some of the well-known makers offered both varieties of the instruments. The tuning of the strings follows that of the violin, making it an ideal "doubling" instrument for the violinist. The latter frequently discover with surprise with what ease they adapt their finger-board technique to the mandolin once they become accustomed to the application of the plectrum to the plucking of the strings.

The mandolin has been around in its present, little-changed shape since the middle ages, and in common with many of similar lineage stems from the parenthood of the lute, which in itself has complex origins and is commented on in its own section.

Whole families of the instrument conforming with similarity to the violin range are known and much loved for their performances of a very wide repertoire of music of many styles, the mandolin's big sister, the mandola, is even more like the cittern and fits well into ensembles with guitar or banjo. The type used by the Spanish "Tuna" groups is called a bandurria, and is used as a melodic instrument accompanied by guitars in their songs, sometimes sentimental, sometimes jovial, but always heartfelt.

Figure 5   Flat-backed Mandolin

Mediaeval Fiddle

Violinists playing this fiddle for the first time may have to make some adjustments to their normal posture since their contact with the different body shape will need to be compensated for. After this, and some players adjust very quickly, there should be few technical complications because to all intents and purposes it is the same instrument. The origins of the fiddle go back many centuries before our Dark Ages and they were shaped in just about every form known to geometry. This instrument was not always played tucked under the chin as is customary with the violin of today, but sometimes held against the chest or even inverted and held vertically like a miniature violoncello.

Bows were also more reminiscent of the type with which arrows are fired, perhaps not surprisingly, and held underhand, in the case of the "inverted" hold. Far less complex in outline, this fiddle is more in line with the Arab instruments which are so frequently to be seen in early manuscripts of France and Spain. The model used for the example we are going to make is one of a pair which may be seen in the company of various instruments of the Middle Ages depicted in the Portico de la Gloria, the entrance to the Cathedral of Santiago de Compostela. It is arguably one of the finest pieces of sculpture to chronicle the instruments of its age, and has been the study of generations of instrument makers. In June 1990 I was honoured to be helping to set up a new museum/workshop attached to the Cathedral for the purpose of replicating the instruments of this famous arch.

By making overall percentage divisions or multiplications it is possible to create either small-scale models for junior players or a viola if there is need for one.

Figure 6   Mediaeval Fiddle

Gothic Harp

Of the many historic instruments depicted in the work of the great masters of painting, few are better known than the artist Hieronymus Bosch. Apart from his fascinating and imaginative surrealism, his draughtsmanship is superb, such that one may almost use his pictures as a working drawing. Featured on the right wing of his tryptich entitled "The Garden of Earthly Delights", there is a quintet of juxtaposed instruments, one of which is the harp featured in this book. I have stood in front of the original in The Prado, Madrid, and remained transfixed for many heartbeats trying to take in the huge canvas and all that it might convey. Even to isolate one tiny portion in order to study the detail was a lengthy and ecstatic experience, leaving me determined to go back one day and drink-in the whole wonderful, crazy, diffusion of mediaeval "Dali-ism".

The harp is another good example of a simple, ancient instrument, as uncomplicated as the bow, except that it gradually benefitted from the development of a sophisticated and powerful soundbox. There are numerous well-known styles of harp which have become fashionable recently in folk-cum-classical circles, and although they are very popular, I find them somewhat artless and in-elegant for my personal taste, although perhaps well-suited to symbolize certain dark beverages that need to project macho appeal.

My choice for you is this graceful and well-proportioned piece of Gothic harmony straight from the hand of a great artist.

Figure 7   Gothic Harp

Classic Guitar

This is one of the world's great all-time favourite musical instruments. It is inexpensive, playable, (in rudimentary terms) by almost anybody, portable and unobtrusive. Of course if one simply uses the word "guitar" it can mean many things. I have described elsewhere at great length, contemporary so-called "pop guitar" playing, and it is not necessary to labour the point further or to lend undeserved importance to the subject.

My concern is with the classic guitar, which in itself needs some qualifying definition. It is assumed that we speak of the instrument which has been used by serious musicians for some five centuries and whose ethnic origins are Spanish.

The most prolific period for the repertoire of the classic guitar was from about 1780 to about 1900. Not all of the output would be received with acclaim by contemporary guitarists, but it is still a sound basis for study administered by expert tutors, or if it comes to that, even for self-tuition. The list of guitarist-composers of that period is extensive, and available more appropriately elsewhere, but if some research is undertaken, it may be found that guitars used by the majority of the performers in the earlier part of that period were of the type made by the makers Lacote and Panormo. Interestingly, the former was French and the latter an Italian, who claimed on his label to be "The only maker of guitars in the Spanish style". I suppose he didn't need to add: "outside Spain, that is!"

I have chosen this era and this style on which to base my classic guitar for its size, since it has a small enough body to be embraced by a lady or a junior, whilst not excluding the experienced player. For the same reason I have chosen to reduce the scale length, although if a "grown-up" size is required, it should not be beyond the ability of an average maker to increase this up to a scale length of say, 630 mm, but do study the section on "Fretting without tears" before redesigning the neck.

I also chose this guitar because it has such grace and refinement about its line, all of which is reflected in the distinction of the tone available from a really well-crafted example.

Figure 8   Classic Guitar

Figure 8a   Back view of Classic Guitar

2. Basic Tools Required

Abrasives: Garnet paper, fine grades. Wire wool, fine grades.

Bench: About 1 metre by 1/2 metre.

Bending Iron: Electric, or make your own. See Chapter 3, "Some Devices to Make".

Bevel Gauge: Standard joiners' type.

Brace and Bits.

Calipers: Outside type up to 25 mm capacity.

Chisels: Up to 25 mm for paring, trimming etc. Miniature chisels for cutting rose in soundboards. Small scraper types for turning tuning-pegs.

Clamps: Various sizes and quantities, depending on instrument.

Drill Bits: Metric and imperial sizes needed in some cases.

Drill Brace: Light engineering type. Archimedes spiral is useful.

Electric Drill: In the case of instruments with many strings.

Files: Needle type, various sections, for trimming fancy apertures.

Glue Pot and brushes: See Chapter 9, "Adhesives" for alternative.

Knives: Scalpel or model type.

Lathe: To make tuning-pegs, but not essential since these may be purchased.

Marking gauge: Standard joinery type.

Measuring Equipment: Steel rule. Straight edge. Vernier caliper, vernier thicknesser or see Chapter 3, "Some Devices to Make".

Planes: Standard smoothing. Low angle block.

Rasps: Flat and half round.

Reamers: Check tapers required according to particular instrument.

Saws: Hand-, tenon-, bow-, (or coping-), fret- and junior hacksaw.

Scrapers: Two-handed or cabinet type, preferably both.

Spokeshave: Flat and concave.

Try Square: Engineer's combination if available.

Vice: Standard bench type or special purpose.

3. Some Devices to Make

List of Devices:

Sanding blocks   Scraper plane
Sanding table   Peg-hole reamer
Bending iron   Peg-trimmer
Bridge clamps

Sanding blocks

Always use a sanding block as a support to the paper for the sake of economy as well as efficiency. In advocating a variety of shapes and sizes in accordance with the particular task, I also recommend making the sizes of blocks relevant to the paper size. If, for example, the paper is A4, and it seems most frequently to be, then a suitably sized block might utilize a third or a quarter of the sheet. As for the application, insert one edge of the paper into the slot, passing it around and under the pad and bringing the remainder up at the side of the block where it is retained by gripping with the fingers. It works very well in practice.

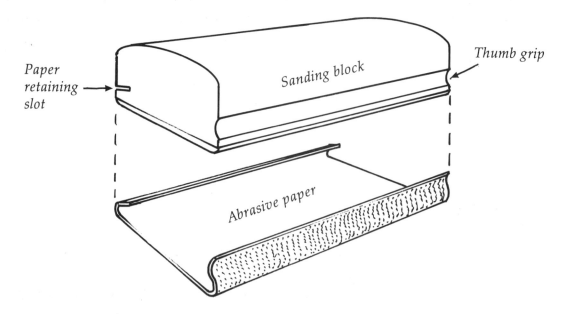

The type of block used in the process of jointing as mentioned in Chapter 4, "Tricks of the Trade" uses double sided tape to attach the abrasive paper to one side, or to two opposite sides. Since its function is to produce an absolutely straight and square edge for jointing, it follows that it must be absolutely straight and square itself. Again, with reference to best use of the abrasive sheet it makes sense to prepare a block for this purpose of 50 mm × 50 mm × 300 mm approximately, thus one sheet will make four sides for this block. As already mentioned, only one or two sides are covered with paper because the side resting on the table, or shooting-board, needs to be smooth and impart as little friction as possible.

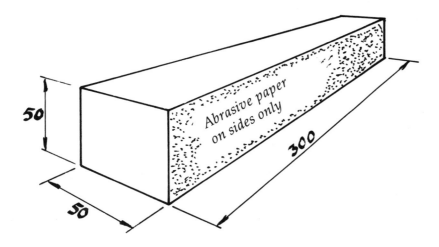

Figure 10   Sanding Block for Jointing

The double sided tape is also useful for sticking abrasive papers to odd-shaped pieces, even sticks of dowel or strips of plywood. They are almost cost-free and just as effective as rasps and files, and in any case the latter are rarely available in shapes or sizes to suit an instrument maker.

Sanding Table

A frequent need to produce a flat plane, (speaking in the geometrical sense, of course) over a relatively large area calls for special care.

It calls for a reversal of the normal application of taking an abrasive to the workpiece; in other words, taking the workpiece to the abrasive. Little more needs be said except for what may not be obvious already, that is, make sure the sanding table is big enough in area to permit lateral movement of the workpiece as it is "scrubbed" across its surface. Make the table from material which retains its flatness under duress. A batten fixed along one underside-edge will help to keep it in place if it is used on a bench-top; better still, if it is simultaneously fixed in a vice.

31

Bending Iron

Before the days of sophisticated, thermostatically controlled, electric bending irons, the luthier took his slender ribs and applied them to the hot stove-pipe, or so I am told, and I see no reason to dispute this. Of course there would be little in the way of fine control of temperature, but no doubt with experience the hot chimney could be utilized effectively.

I find the standard off-the-shelf electric bending iron far from ideal in several ways. It stands vertically, unless you have some substantial upright post to which it may be attached, and the anchorage of the iron itself, being at its bottom end, frequently leads to loosening at the joint. This means instability which worsens each time pressure is applied, and that is what bending irons get. Add to this the waiting time for the iron to achieve working heat, and the need to protect the electric gadgetry from water, in the case of working wet wood, and in my analysis it has not been perfected. Yes, I know, you know someone who has used one of these for years with no trouble, etc., but the fact remains that in principle it has shortcomings. Mine has fewer.

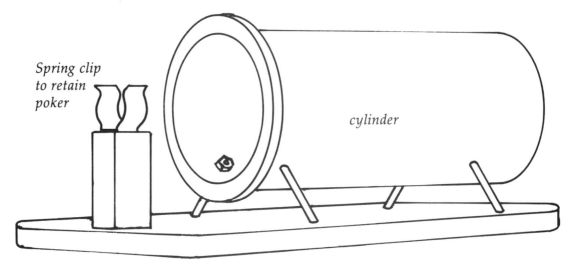

Spring clip to retain poker

cylinder

Figure 11   Bending Iron

This is made from a cylinder liner acquired from a scrap merchant. It is supported on four screwed bolts which act as legs. A poker powered by a gas cylinder is fixed by a spring-clip mounted on a block of wood. I obtained my poker at a jumble-sale, and the gas cylinder is a relic from camping days. Total cost about one-twentieth of a bought iron.

But wait. In this strange era when most people's conversation begins on the topic of money, shouldn't we expect a cheaper thing to be inferior? Consider the function of our home-spun iron. It rests, projecting, on a bench, temporarily clamped for stability. Within seconds I can have the tube up to "spit-back" heat, and readily controllable through a wide temperature range. I can press down on the iron rather than pushing or pulling, which means directly against its support, rather than across it, so that weakening of its anchorage is unlikely in its normal use. And as for running-costs, they are so low as to be almost negligible. There is a flanged rim running around the end of the tube which gives a positive guide against which the piece to be bent may be located during the bending operation ensuring parallelism and a consistent radial shape. So, there you have a choice. You may buy a "special-purpose" appliance which is almost ideal, or speculate a little time and imagination, and make one of your own to do exactly what you need.

Bridge Clamps

So-called because of their use in clamping a bridge to a guitar front, but of considerable use in any situation where a long reach is required. They are quick to apply and are unlikely to cause damage through over-tightening, particularly since it is usual to face the jaws with leather, cork, or what-you-will. If metal bars are not easily accessible then a good quality multi-ply will do.

Figure 12   Bridge Clamp

The jaws and cam lever are made from hardwood. Clamping faces cork faced. Pins are mild steel. Bar of mild steel or aluminium.

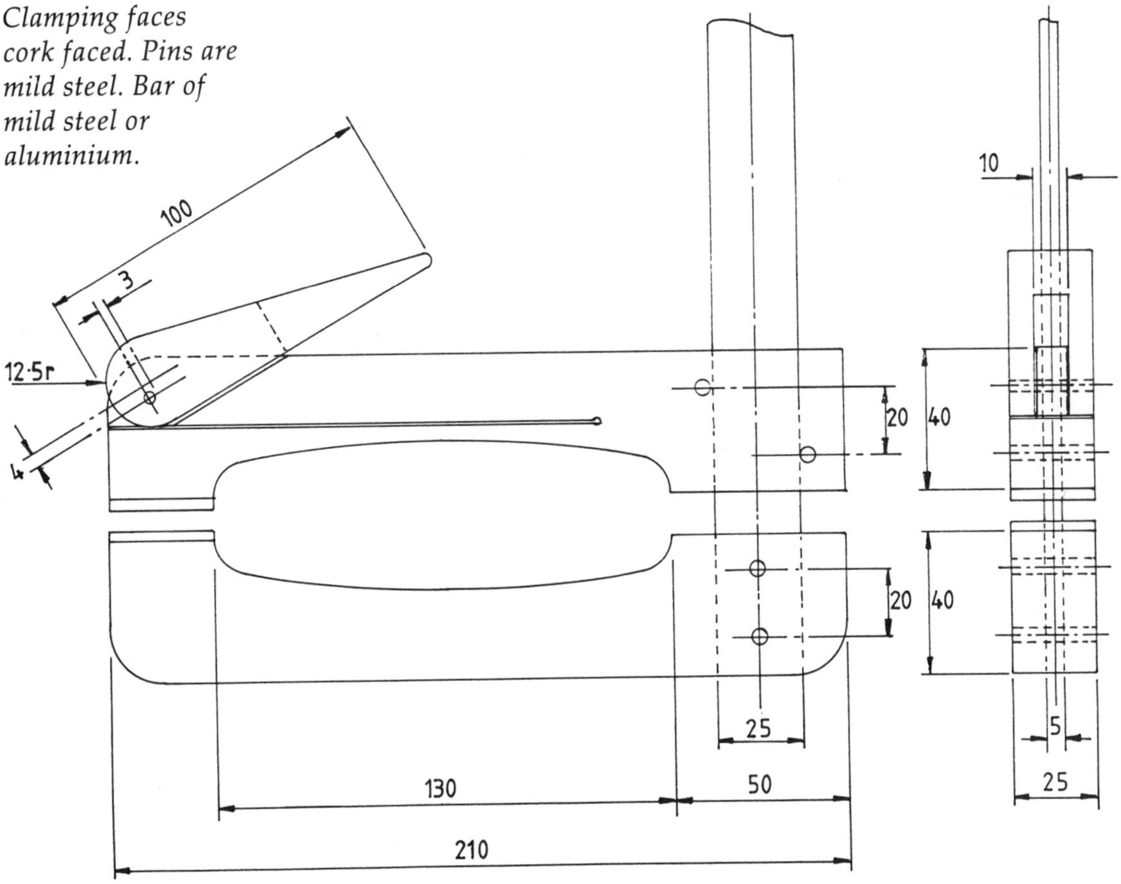

Scraper Plane

This was born out of the need to plane and scrape wide ribs for a guitar. The blade is a standard cabinet scraper but with the edge ground at 45 degrees and burred over in conventional manner. Perhaps a little more detail is necessary for those not used to preparing a blade in this fashion.

Assuming the blade has been ground at 45 degrees:

1. Hone it on a stone to produce a chisel-sharp edge.
2. Place the blade, sharp edge towards you with the bevel down, on the bench.
3. Rest a ticketer, or some other hardened steel artefact, on the blade and, stroking from side to side, "draw" the edge of the sharpened blade by applying the very slightest of pressure. This should improve the sharpness of the edge and prepare it for "burring-over".
4. Hold it firmly in a vice with the sharp edge projecting vertically, sharp edge towards you, and stroke the ticketer along the edge gradually lowering it until it is horizontal. This should produce a "burr" which is the characteristic of this type of tool.

Figure 13   Scraper plane

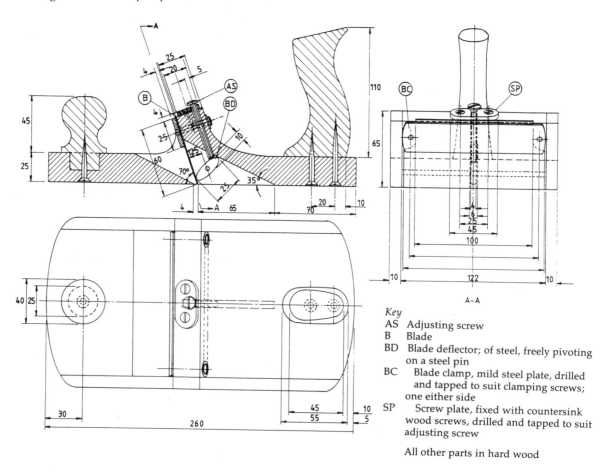

Key
AS Adjusting screw
B   Blade
BD Blade deflector; of steel, freely pivoting on a steel pin
BC Blade clamp, mild steel plate, drilled and tapped to suit clamping screws; one either side
SP Screw plate, fixed with countersink wood screws, drilled and tapped to suit adjusting screw

All other parts in hard wood

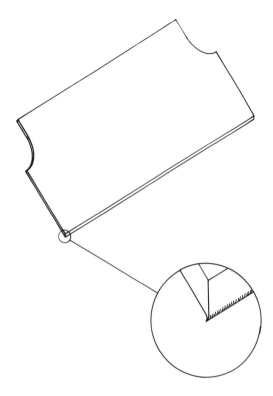

Figure 14   Scraper Iron

I often use the blade by hand in the manner of the traditional cabinet scraper and it performs very satisfactorily. But its true purpose is achieved when mounted in the plane, for then you will not only obtain a wonderful finish, but a flat surface into the bargain. If not, something is wrong either in the sharpening, the fitting, or the adjustment of the blade. Persevere!

Peg-hole Reamer

There is an obvious need to match tapered tuning-pegs with the holes into which they will be inserted, so logically this item and its companion, the peg-trimmer, are best thought of as a pair. As will readily be seen, it is advantageous to make the reamer first, since then it becomes the reference for matching the peg-trimmer.

Using a bar, of suitable diameter, either high-speed steel for a durable reamer or mild-steel for a cheaper one, turn a taper to match the pegs. Grind or file off one half of the tapered bar to form a "D" section. Square-off the end to fit a tap-wrench or other device.

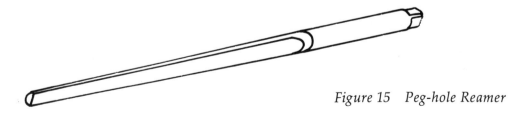

Figure 15   Peg-hole Reamer

Peg-trimmer

Whether the maker possesses a lathe, or not, this device facilitates the marrying of the tuning-pegs and their corresponding holes. The following method should result in a perfect matching.

Take a hardwood block as shown in the illustration and drill a pilot hole of the smallest diameter of the peg-reamer, either the one you have made from the details above, or from one you have otherwise acquired.

Enter the reamer into the hole until it is fully inserted. This is assuming, of course, that the pegs to be trimmed are of the diameter of the reamer. If smaller, then the hole is made to suit. Mark the saw-lines, following the illustration, and cut out the corner of the block to expose the hole. The aperture should be a parallel slot if it has been cut properly, if not, adjust by taking away surplus material. Obviously, it is possible at this stage to overdo it and render the device useless. When the aperture is clear and parallel, apply the blade, sharpened as shown, and fix it with two small clamps. Some adjustment may be necessary in order to get a clean cut, and the principle of "a little, often", is the best advice.

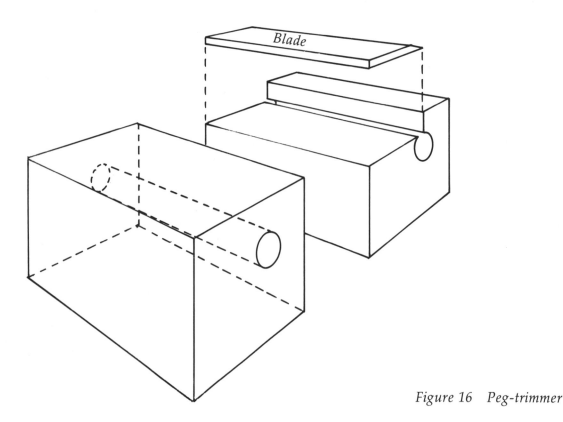

Figure 16   Peg-trimmer

4. Tricks of the Trade

What pleasure there is in coming across some easy way out of a knotty problem, or discovering a method of producing some effect by means of a secure, dare we say, "foolproof" process. Know-how comes along various routes and not always ones that are immediately familiar, although some of the real gems of ingenuity when presented for the first time bring a "knew it all the time" reaction about them.

Take the jointing of a two piece soundboard, or if it comes to that, producing any straight joint between two pieces of similar length and thickness. Assuming you have first planed the faces to be joined on a shooting-board, then, to ensure perfect matching faces every time, give them the following treatment: having prepared a block according to the one detailed in Chapter 3, "Some Devices to Make" proceed to lay one of the work-pieces on top of the other with its joint-face overhanging, then with firm and consistent pressure rub the sanding block along the joint-face. This should square-up and true-up the work-piece providing the block is not wobbled or rocked as the passes are made. Reverse the work-pieces and repeat the sanding process on the second piece and, (in theory!) you should have as good a joint as it is possible to make.

Several instruments use wood in a form produced by bending. This is usually done by applying heat to soften the fibres, then allowing the piece to cool whilst retaining its bent shape. I try to use dry heat for this, (having gone to a great deal of trouble to dry it out in the first place, I am not too keen on re-acquainting it with moisture!), however if it is stubborn, and some dense woods can be rather wilful, some water may help.

This is the method I use: using the home-made bending iron, constructed as described, bring it to a heat sufficient to spit back if water is dripped onto it. Locate the central point of the required curve in the work-piece against the top centre of the iron and try bending it after sufficient contact is made to soften the fibres. You will feel this yield point provided you are sensitive to slight movements. Keep the pressure constant and try to achieve the bend required by eye before checking against the mould or template. Increase the area of contact if needed by rocking the work-piece and *not* by sliding it to and fro. The action mentioned latterly tends to "iron" the wood and brings about a brittleness in its surface. Your iron will preferably have a rim or flange running around it which should be used as a register against which the edge of the work-piece is brought to ensure the parallelism of the bend and its angular uniformity. This is essential to maintain the squareness of the body between the top and sides, back and sides, or what-have-you.

In the case of an unwilling material, rather than resorting to boiling, (!) which is advocated by at least one "authority" on instrument making, I recommend the placing of a wet, but well-wrung-out, *clean*, cloth on the hot iron against which the work-piece is pressed. The result is the temporary impregnation of the wood with steam which should help to ease it into shape whilst helping to protect against scorching. If your material is persistently obdurate, soak it in water overnight, or longer if need be, prior to bending, but I still recommend the wet cloth on the iron to ensure that plenty of localised steam is created. Do not be surprised if the bent member tries to assume its original shape after being bent, since wood has a memory and needs to be restricted, preferably by placing in its mould or held against some pattern whilst it cools or "cures". There is certainly no point in trying to force an unwilling piece into some shape and hoping its adjoining members will hold it in place when glued. You are unlikely to be lucky and may have an instrument most horribly mis-shapen as the various forces begin to battle against each other.

Quite apart from the know-how of tool application, and the acquisition of the appropriate wood, assuming you know what shape it must eventually become, there is the fundamental requirement to hold it securely in position whilst working upon it. Few pieces offer more difficulty in this respect than planing thin soundboards, or ribs, sides, backs, etc. It is normal to hold the piece by clamping at one end and planing away from, rather than towards, the clamp. This obviously needs care and can be frustrating in the case of difficult cross-grained pieces which demand "one-direction" planing. So why bother with clamps, get out the double-sided tape and stick the piece to the bench-top! Surprised at this advice? Don't be, I use any means at my disposal to achieve the required result and this includes all kinds of modern technology that some purists would shun. I believe that if the instrument, or any part of it, is satisfactory in its function and that its appearance is in keeping with the high standards normally expected of such artefacts, then the means by which it was achieved is irrelevant to the player. Efficiency and economy are different questions and are of concern only when the matter of time and its costs become pertinent.

5. About Reading Drawings

The very word "drawing" means different things to different people, from artists to architects, from finger-painters to engineers.

As a young man, I was trained in engineering and steered in the direction of the Drawing Office. This is not so surprising since I was born in the Black Country and come from a long line of engineers. One of my mentors at college was Jim Kent, a much revered lecturer, to whom a whole room was devoted in the Birmingham Science Museum to display his wonderfully reproduced scale models of ancient machinery. Jim Kent was one of the most exacting masters I ever met, and although he seldom gave compliments, one felt that any comment he made in criticism of one's work was honest and encouraging.

Here I learned not only the principles of meticulous precision, but the sacred duty to observe accurate communication of technical data to whomsoever should flatter the draughtsman by referring to his drawing. British Standard, First Angle Projection, is what we were taught. Occasionally, for the experience, we used American Third Angle Projection, but this was not to be indulged in as a serious study as anything as "new fangled" as this, and representative of something foreign, to boot, was not to be regarded with trust. In any case, the toolmakers and production engineers were, and probably still are, more accustomed to the former system. I shall not dwell further on these aspects of technical drawing, (and there are many more!), but suffice it to say that all the principles which follow are those concerned with First Angle Projection.

First consider the draughtsman's job. He must convey all the necessary dimensions of an object through at least three related views. Very few objects may be shown by the use of only two. One may refer to the three views as: Front Elevation, Side Elevation and Plan. It can be readily seen that in the case of a geographical map, or "plan", only the dimensions of latitude and longitude may be measured. Any reference to altitude may only be shown by contour lines, calling for a certain amount of imagination, but still not showing an actual altitude outline. Of course this is a perfectly adequate system for the purpose of place location, but it would not be sufficient for a structural project.

Let us consider a simple example. Imagine trying to convey to a potter, the shape required for a domestic mug, if one only had a plan view. The drawing would simply appear as a circle with a rectangle attached. The potter would have no idea of the shape of the mug or its height. Similar problems occur if only side and front views are given.

In this case one is presented with what appears to be a cube with a handle attached. Thus, one appreciates just how important are the three inter-related views.

If an article is made up of several parts the draughtsman may need to verify the design and compatibility of the components by producing an assembly drawing. This is usually accompanied by detail drawings which show dimensions of the component parts. This is to try to obviate confusion which might occur with hidden detail. To bring about the production of any article by this method requires experience on the part of the draughtsman and the maker.

So, having accepted that three views are required, let us proceed to the way in which they will be related to each other on the drawing. Let us return to our mug. Suppose I pick up the mug in my right hand. If I raise it to eye-level I assume I am looking at the Front View, or, Front Elevation, if you prefer. It appears thus:

Mug
Front view

Figure 17

If I rotate it until I can see the handle in the centre of the mug I have a Side View, or Side Elevation. As below:

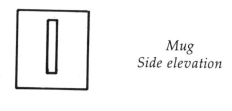

Mug
Side elevation

Figure 18

Turning the mug as if to see inside, I assume this is looking from above and therefore refer to the view as the Plan.

Mug
Plan

Figure 19

It now remains to arrange the three views in such a way that will convey the relativity of the lines and dimensions. Choosing a location above and to the left of centre of my sheet of drawing paper, I produce the Front View first, to reveal the handle at its side. I then imagine I am looking at the mug facing the side opposite the handle, as shown previously. This view, the Side Elevation, will be shown on the opposite side. That is, put simply, what you see on one side you show on the other.

Similarly, the Plan appears underneath the Front View.

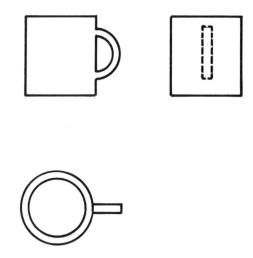

Figure 20   Orthographic arrangement of mug drawing

As I have chosen to view the mug from the side opposite the handle, then, of course, that view would have been placed on the opposite side. In this case the handle is shown in dotted outline to indicate a hidden detail.

We can show the thickness of the clay to be used in this way by showing its interior dimensions in dotted lines. An alternative is to show a Section Drawing, as if it had been cut and exposed. In this case the exposed facets are cross-hatched thus:

Figure 21   Section of mug

Of course, there are many rules governing the production of technical drawings and, sadly, not all of them are observed by some who lazily ignore the need to be fastidious in this exacting medium. Even if a "checker" is employed, occasionally mistakes are overlooked, and this applies to my drawings contained herein. If an error is observed by a reader I should appreciate having my attention drawn to it.

6. Conversion to Imperial Dimensions

Until I was 25 years old I never used metric measurements, apart from academic exercises at school and college to illustrate comparison with the imperial system. Those occasions were usually presented by mature teachers who had themselves been accustomed to the latter, therefore ill-inclined towards recommending a less familiar system. Thus it is that metrication remained available, but rarely used — like the Ordnance Survey Grid Reference, for example, and what a wonderful system that is.

But after considerable experience with continental luthiers, metrics were noticeably more facile for calculating, designing, yes, and taking-off measurements too, than the intellectually-cumbersome imperial method. In any case, as long as one has measuring equipment compatible with that given in the plans, there is no need to convert, from anything, to anything. What is more, one quickly assimilates the other system and adds to one's flexibility. You will notice many people flinch if faced with dividing say, 1 ⅝" by 5. Of course, an engineer would swiftly convert the figure to 1.625, which would make it more manageable, decimalisation itself being a step in the metric direction. I think I can still recite decimal conversions of an inch divided into 32nds, and many 64th divisions, up to four places of decimals. Can't be many of us left. . . Anyway, may I suggest that if you insist on using the imperial system, then use the quick reference chart below, and if the dimension you are after is not shown, divide the millimetres by 25.4 and you have the inch equivalent.

millimetres	inches or millimetres	decimal inches	(nearest fraction)
25.4	1	.039	1/32
50.8	2	.079	5/64
76.2	3	.118	1/8
101.6	4	.157	5/32
127.0	5	.197	3/16
152.4	6	.236	1/4
177.8	7	.275	9/32
203.2	8	.315	5/16
228.6	9	.354	11/32
254.0	10	.394	3/8

7. Fundamentals of Plucked String Acoustics

The study of acoustics is quite ancient. Since the dawn of history man has made music and with his growth of knowledge so has his fascination with the technology of sound production. Whether by accident or by design or by the happy combination of the two, the development of musical instruments has given rise to an entire field of scientific study. Many universities now support faculties devoted entirely to this subject, and to try to cover it in any thorough sense would be beyond the scope of this volume, and in any case, largely superfluous.

Even so, a word or two about the principles may be useful in helping to assess certain features of materials to be selected, or where choice of dimensions for structural members may be critical, etc.

Let us therefore consider the major physical elements which contribute to sound in terms of its volume and quality.

1. The Motivating Agent, or Sound Source

In the case of all of the instruments described in this volume, the Motivating Agent is the string. Strings may be made from many materials and these are described in the section headed "Strings and Fitting Them". The material is an important consideration of course and this is related to its tension, diameter and vibrating length. It may be readily seen that in considering the three latter physical ingredients, a ratio exists. An obvious example is that of a guitar string which is capable of producing one and a half octaves, (at least), by holding the string against the fingerboard, thus shortening the vibrating length without variation of either the diameter or the tension. Unlike say, the piano, which has no means of shortening the strings or varying the tension during performance so it is equipped with strings of differing diameter and length to achieve the correct tension and pitch.

2. Type of Activation

The method used to activate the string also plays an important part in the nature of the sound it produces. For example, a given string will respond quite differently to activation by plucking, striking or bowing. Notice the vast difference between the sounds given by a violin when its strings are either bowed or plucked ("con arco" or "pizzicato", to a violinist.) Compare the majestic tone of a piano played normally, with the result obtained by the somewhat unconventional method of plucking the strings. The characteristic sounds produced by these various means have always been strangely predictable to myself, although I would have difficulty in explaining the logic of this, and I am sure I am not alone in this intuition.

3. The Transmitter, or Bridge

Two basic types of bridge are in general use: that which is fixed to the soundboard, and the other which is held against the soundboard by the pressure of the strings. In the former case, the bridge functions as the anchorage for the strings as well as transmitter. In the second application the strings are usually attached to a tailpiece fitted to the end of the body with the bridge held against the soundboard by pressure exerted by the taut strings. In either case good contact is essential between the three parts, string, bridge and soundboard, otherwise poor transmission will result, to the detriment of potential amplification and tone quality. The design of the bridge is a highly refined subject and each instrument has its own individually developed shape.

4. Responsive Stratum, or Soundboard

In addition to the names shown above, this member may be referred to by various others, such as the top, the table, the vibrating membrane, the diaphragm, etc. Its main purpose is to amplify by responding sympathetically to the vibrations transmitted through the bridge. Apart from the grain and density of the material used for the soundboard, the way it is braced, strutted and secured are major features of design which contribute enormously to the volume and character of the sound produced by the instrument.

Instruments which amplify by resonating or vibrating in response to a motivating agent, such as a soundboard responding to the vibrating of a string are likely to benefit from the provision of a so-called soundhole. This simply permits air into and out of the sound chamber as deformation of the component parts takes place. This airway is not needed in the case of a drum since deformation is undergone by the skin membrane, permitting compression to be distributed over a wide area and within a comparatively large volume.

Nevertheless, a difference in the quality of the tone is discernible if a hole is made in the body of a drum. Following this train of thought, it might make reasonable sense to place the soundhole of the guitar in the rib or even the back, thus leaving the soundboard complete and therefore free to vibrate over as large an area as possible.

Unfortunately we then enter the sensitive area of conventional aesthetics where conformity rules very firmly. Few people are prepared to embrace the unusual where traditional and well-proven precedents exist. And why should they? Then again, let us not forget the motto "Conformity is the enemy of progress".

5. Sound Chamber, or Body

Generally, this part has the major function of supporting the soundboard. In the same way that a speaker in a hi-fi system is held securely in a relatively substantial cabinet. Note that in the latter case the cabinet itself is not resonating, in fact one must take care that it does not have too much responsive potential in case it becomes an absorptive agent and thus reduce the effectiveness of the speaker diaphragm. As a rule it may be assumed that high-density, close-grained hardwoods are selected most often for bodies, and in this respect a relatively wide choice is available, permitting appearance to play an aesthetic part.

6. What is better?

Many inventive ideas have been employed to make plucked-string instruments more efficient. Many different shapes have emerged, many cast aside as failures. Masses of experiments have been carried out to help determine maximum efficacy from the co-ordinated members, each maker generally seeking to improve on earlier systems. It is rare that any discernible progress is made in this respect, due mainly to ambitious experimentalism based on misconceptions or ignorance.

There is now ample information made available from informed and musically inclined scientists who have verified by modern technology the means of getting the best from conventional instruments, obviating unnecessary waste of materials or time. In any case, "improvement" implies change, and we are then faced with the somewhat subjective argument as to whether that change is better or not.

I remember walking with the great Andres Segovia to his taxi after one of those amazing concerts during which I noticed that he had been using a new instrument of a make that was not of his usual choice. "Maestro, I saw that you were using a new guitar this evening", I remarked. "That is so" he replied, without indicating surprise at my clever observation. I ventured further. "I am not sure that this new guitar gives a better sound". "It is certainly giving a greater volume", came the positive response. I gained confidence. "Should that be a major consideration?" I asked, loading his guns unwittingly. "It is necessary because of the nature of *your* society," he quickly replied, at once exonerating himself from the responsibility of anything that might be diminishing to our culture, and planting the liability for the Great Scheme of Things firmly at *my* feet! There was more. . . "Always you make the auditorium bigger. The audience grows bigger. So the sound from the guitar must follow the pattern otherwise it will not be heard. We live in noisy times". The last phrase was uttered ruefully and with a note of pity rather than of anger. I might have felt mildly rebuked, but I didn't. I felt as I had on other occasions in his presence — privileged.

8. Materials

The conversation is unlikely to run dry between luthiers when the subject of materials is encountered, and whether the topic is concerned with the acoustic, structural or decorative function of the part, it is an area where makers have an opportunity to individualize.

Or have they?

Let us consider for a moment the classic guitar. Most players will state a preference for the use of rosewood for the back and sides, book-matched and highly polished. A similar instrument made with a one-piece maple back would not be looked upon with much favour except by a non-conformist. Mind you, it would not require an enormous amount of enquiry to find such a feature in a really fine violin. But try to find one made in rosewood. I dare you to ask!

The reasons for this state of affairs are complex involving considerations of appearance, colour, fashion, texture, acoustic puissance, working properties, availability, cost, and that trusty, old-fashioned, die-hard, *tradition*! I do not readily accept the philosophical empiricism of "trial and error" techniques, nor do I have much faith in the romantic notion that "if it looks right, it is right". This does not mean that I do not "try" and that I do not "err". On the contrary. And as a rule I keep in mind the appearance of the article for reasons of aesthetic wholesomeness. However, without scientific rationalism added to our imagination and intuition, our efforts are likely to be somewhat diminished in effective progress.

Let us first attempt to categorize the material elements. Although some parts of an instrument are multi-functional, in this respect it is their primary contribution which is under consideration. Soundboards, for example, are very plain in appearance being generally made from spruce or something similar. This probably accounts in some ways for decorated sound-holes, fancy bridges and ornamental purfling to compensate for its relatively large and uninspiring area. It may be assumed then that we choose material for this part for its quality as an acoustic member. With this as a general basis the list below may be used as a guide to aid selection of materials, but only with reference to the instruments which appear in this book and not necessarily to other varieties. Items shown in **bold** indicate those most generally preferred.

SOUNDBOARD

EUROPEAN SPRUCE, SITKA SPRUCE, FIR, CEDAR

The above applies to all of the instruments, although for "austerity" models 3 mm plywood functions adequately on psaltery, rote and dulcimer. The Compostelan lute has a calf- or goat-skin soundboard.

BACKS, SIDES, RIBS

CHERRY, CHESTNUT, LABURNUM, MAHOGANY, MAPLE, PADAUK, **ROSEWOOD**, SYCAMORE, WALNUT (AMERICAN OR EUROPEAN), YEW

Yes, I know there will be purist eyebrows raised at the idea of using mahogany, or padauk, for early instruments, but I am concerned with readily available alternatives at the moment.

NECKS

CYPRESS, MAHOGANY, **MAPLE**, POPLAR, SYCAMORE, CEDAR

Consider the density when choosing; a large member may present problems of imbalance if a heavy material is used.

INTERNAL BRACES, LININGS, STRUCTURAL BLOCKS

FIR, LIME, **SPRUCE**, WILLOW

A relatively short list this, due to the requirement of strength coupled with low density.

FINGERBOARDS

EBONY, MAPLE, PEAR, ROSEWOOD, SYCAMORE

The major need from this part is that it be durable under the abrasion of fingers pressing strings against it, but it also reinforces the neck against warping.

BRIDGES

EBONY, MAPLE, PEAR, ROSEWOOD, SYCAMORE

It must resist splitting and accept constant, but not consistent, pressure, as it supports the vibrating strings.

TUNING PEGS (WOODEN)

CHESTNUT, **EBONY**, LABURNUM, LAUREL, MAPLE, PEAR, ROSEWOOD

Note, in the case of the psaltery and harp, the tuning is via steel "wrest pins" purchasable from most music stores.

Naturally, when appraising an instrument as a whole, its appearance must play an important part. Colour is therefore of great concern, and although at a glance woods may present a generally brown aura, one does not need to search very hard to discover many variations in hue as well as grain pattern. Whether using a similar colour overall or using some contrast, it is prudent to limit the choice to as few as possible, related or not, in order to preserve a tasteful and co-ordinated appearance.

Spectacular grain patterns may be enhanced by book-matching. This is a technique well-known to cabinet makers where a dramatically figured piece is split and opened like two pages in a book. Attention is drawn to the figure by the resulting mirrored effect. See this in the backs of the violin family and good class guitars. There is no reason why the technique should not be used also in the psaltery, rote, dulcimer or mandolin.

Having decided which woods are going to be used, it only remains to locate the appropriate piece. For this it is necessary to know from which part of the tree it is taken since the run of the grain is an essential feature of the particular member. Usually we have our eye on structural or acoustic considerations in this respect.

Figure 22   Stages in the production of a book-matched soundboard

After quartering a log, boards are sawn radially from the log. Bark, cambium and dead heart wood are discarded and the remainder is left as sound wood with annular rings at right angles to the sawn faces. A pair of consecutive boards will thus produce book-matching when glued central edge to central edge.

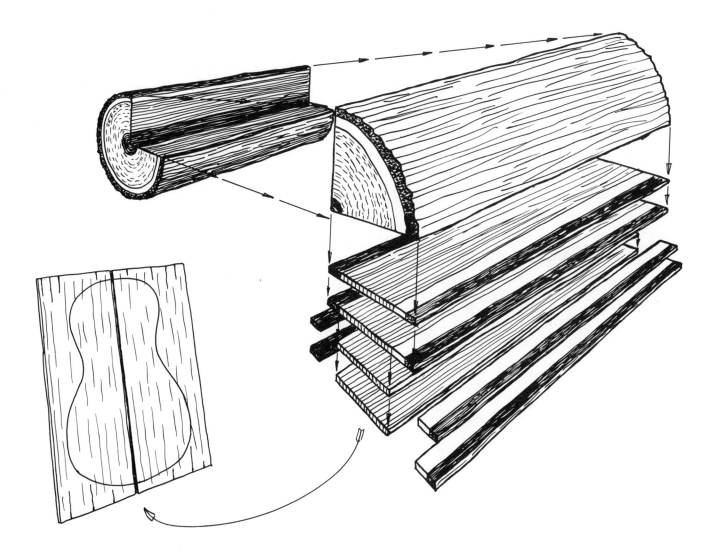

9. Adhesives

Given that most glues do the job of sticking things together providing the methods advised by the manufacturer are observed, in general, I categorize them in two simple ways: either they are reversible, or they are not.

Instruments get broken or sometimes need to be adjusted making it necessary to dismantle certain parts in order to carry out the repair. Hardly any modern adhesive will revert by softening to permit disassembly of parts, in fact many are promoted by emphasizing their indestructability. I do not intend to dwell here on descriptions or techniques of the application of glues which have become commonly used, since in any case they are freely available at many retail outlets.

I am inclined to use "Scotch" glue, or "Hot" glue or "Animal" glue or "Hoof-and-hide" or whatever else you may know it by, simply because with a little care the joints fixed by this glue may be relatively easily released without damage and also replaced. Try that with Epoxy!

Animal glue comes as solid or in pearls (made from hooves, hides and tendons of animals) to be soaked in water, heated to liquefy and applied warm. If you have not used this method before, it probably sounds rather messy. And it can be. However since my last book, "Make and Play a Lute", there has been a significant addition to the wide variety of available adhesives. I will come to that in a moment, but let me describe a method of using animal glue.

As described earlier, it may be bought in slab or pearl form; either way, if there is a choice, take the one lightest in colour, to render a well-made joint even less visible. A double pot is needed to "cook" the glue and although a special glue-pot may be obtained I use a small saucepan immersed in an old electric kettle which I find very satisfactory. Using the inner pot to hold the solid glue, add to it about twice as much water, by volume, and leave it to soak. If convenient leave overnight and cover to keep out dust and foreign matter. Insert the pot into the water contained in the outer container and heat.

Consistency of the glue may need to be adjusted to bring it to a working state. This is a matter of experience and, up to a point, personal preference. The glue does need to run freely from a knife or spatula and not hold on to the knife when withdrawn from the pot. This would indicate a need for more water. Use hot water for topping-up, of course. Naturally, the water content is reduced as heating continues, requiring replenishment from time to time when a lengthy gluing session is undertaken. If the heat is turned off, the glue will then gradually solidify with cooling, but it may be readily rejuvenated by re-heating. Do not forget to keep the glue covered when not in use.

It is best to gently warm any parts which are to be glued just prior to their joining in order to take full advantage of one of the features of this wonderful glue — that of delayed setting time — enabling alignment of the parts without panic. If a mistake occurs it is a simple matter to warm the area of the joint and insert a hot, wet knife into the joint in order to separate for re-alignment.

Franklins have recently produced a hide glue which is used in liquid form straight from a square bottle. This can be used in a similar way to the traditional type except that it does not need to be heated. I do warm it a little to increase its flow if the day is cold, but generally it is as easy to use as the common P.V.A. glues. I have also reversed it many times, treating it in the same manner as conventional hide glue and it behaves in the same way. Franklins also produces a superior aliphatic adhesive called Titebond which has been around for some years.

Table of Selected Glues and their Properties

TYPE	CON- STITUENTS	SETS BY	FORM	PREPARATION	COMMENTS
Aliphatic (Yellow Glue) such as 'Titebond'	Polyvinyl Acetate in modified form	Absorption (1 hour)	Liquid	None	Less tendency to creep. Similar to but generally superior to P.V.A.
Animal	Hoof, Hide and Tendon	Evaporation (Hours)	Granules	Soak in water. Heat to liquefy	Reversible by re-heating. High in strength but low in moisture resistance
Casein such as 'Cascamite One-Shot'	Milk Based	Evaporation (Hours)	Powder	Mixed with water	Irreversible. High in moisture resistance
Epoxy such as 'Devcon'	Resin and Catalyst	Chemical Action (Minutes)	Semi-Liquid	Mixing of the two parts	Very strong bond. Heat and waterproof. In some cases reversible with paint stripper
Franklins Hide Glue	Animal protein	Evaporation (Hours)	Liquid	None	As animal glue but easier application
P.V.A. such as Evo-Stik 'W'	Polyvinyl Acetate	Absorption (Hours)	Liquid	Some may be diluted with water otherwise used straight from container	It tends to 'creep' under load, dislikes heat and damp

10. Finishing

By the ambivalent term, "finishing", the craftsman can mean either the completion of a project or, more usually, the varnishing process. In this section I wish to deal with both senses of the word, so, taking them in progressive order let us deal with the penultimate process prior to applying whatever may be the surface treatment. Regardless of the choice of coating, and this will be dealt with in detail, some fundamentals must be considered with regard to the preparation of the surface.

1. Remove all traces of glue. This can best be seen as either an abrupt change in colour or a hard shiny area on the surface.
2. Remove any tool marks and scratches left by abrasive papers. Cabinetmaker's steel or glass scrapers may be best for this, followed up with fine papers and steel wool.
3. Remove greasy or oily patches made by fingers, etc. This may need a degreasant in the form of a spirit or thinners to remove all traces.

As a general rule I prefer not to change the natural colours by staining, in fact I have never used stain in any instrument. Many luthiers, particularly those who make the violin family are accustomed to colouring the wood either by staining with dyes or by the application of coloured varnishes. I have no personal experience of this and in any case there is no need for its use on the instruments described herein.

Varnishes used for surface finish on musical instruments generally are either spirit- or oil-based. Taking the former first, we are speaking of a methylated spirit in which has been dissolved a resin, such as shellac. Care must be taken in applying several lightly brushed coats, building up to a smooth surface, obtained by rubbing down each layer as they are applied, when dry. The method of "French" polishing, using a cloth to apply the shellac, is dealt with expertly in several books specially written on the subject (see Bibliography). Most spirit varnishes which contain shellac have the effect of imparting a yellowish colour to the wood, particularly if it is a pale material. This will depend on the varnish itself and they may vary in the density of colouring. It is not an effect I like and so I never use this finish.

Oil varnish comes in a variety of colours and some makers prefer to use this facility to colour and finish simultaneously. Violins are a good example of where the traditional amber hues of great violins are part of the character of the instruments. I still prefer to use the natural colour of the wood, although it must be said that I would be unlikely to attract a potential customer with a violin in natural sycamore and spruce colours. In any case, most oils, will gradually oxidise to a darker yellowish tone. Walnut oil is lighter than most and affects the natural colours less. Whichever oil is chosen for the finish, the maker must be prepared to spend almost as long in applying the finish as it takes to build the instrument, since a dozen or more coats are needed with maybe some weeks between coats to ensure each is dry before re-application.

The craftsmen with the stamina to finish their instruments in this manner will be rewarded with a durable, and marvellously grain-enhancing appearance.

After applying a generous film of warm oil to the wood, rubbing in follows, using a cloth wrapped around some suitable pad. The friction will help to keep the oil warm and this must be maintained until all the oil has been absorbed. Almost no lustre will be discernible at this point and maybe very little until three or more similar applications are completed (depending on the nature of the oil). Any "sweat" marks which appear as saturation is reached should be removed by wiping away with a meths-soaked rag.

There are many suitable varieties of special varnishes available through commercial outlets which have their own special needs, and upon these I do not need to dwell. I believe I have used every type of proprietary varnish available with varying success, but for ease of application and a reliable finish, my chosen method is as follows:

1. Lightly cover the surface with a spirit varnish, or a shellac sealer and rub down when hard with steel wool, 000 grade, or finer.   2. Repeat 1.

3. Inspect under a bright tungsten light to check for any flaws before next stage. Even very minor scratches may show through the final finish so now is the time for a little more patience.

4. Apply wax polish of the type refined for good quality cabinet work. This leaves a hard film of only microns in thickness which is all that is necessary to produce a shine when buffed with a soft, clean duster. The more coats of wax, the more buffing, the more shine.

Whilst it is not possible with wax to obtain the high shine achievable with synthetic lacquers, there is a warm wholesome feel about this finish which is easy to produce and it allows a certain appearance of "life" in the wood. It also seems a little more in keeping with the early type of instrument as distinct from say, the treacly gloss finish associated with modern instruments. Oil finishes, such as might be found on a Cremonese violin, can be very beautiful, but also very demanding of skill, patience and time, particularly the latter, since the drying time is extensive in conditions of humidity normal to Great Britain.

Here are some observations with regard to specific instruments:

Do not varnish or wax any fingerboard such as on the Appalachian dulcimer, mandolin, fiddle, lute or guitar. The lyre and mediaeval lute are excellent vehicles for painted finishes or even pyrography for the more artistic craftsman. Be careful to avoid touching the wheel of the hurdy-gurdy with the fingers since any greasy contamination renders it detrimental to its acceptance of the rosin for the friction needed to vibrate the strings.

Finally, a philosophical attitude to finishing might be acquired by following the words of Michelangelo who advised *the patient perseverance of the removal of every superfluity*. So, get out your magnifying glass and persevere!

Decoration

This term is taken to mean any additional feature used to enhance the appearance of the instrument, in some cases the decoration may also incorporate reinforcement or structural support in some way. A good example, serving both needs, is the purfling around the periphery of the guitar soundboard. This serves to decorate the edge and protect the soft material from which soundboards are usually made. The implication is that hardwood, or in some cases, fibre, or plastics, is therefore a better choice as purfling. I must say that I find the former more desirable, not only aesthetically, but the appearance of the final result is generally preferable.

Whilst some measure of individuality is afforded the maker in the choice of decoration or inlay, it is best not to stray too far from the traditional path, if it is desired to have one's work accepted by the conventional player. We are all victims of conditioning to some extent, and musicians have expectations of appearances as well as playability from instruments. I have seen some examples of inlaying that put the well-endowed Christmas tree to shame, and others which were not only over-decorated but with stick-on plastic laminates usually reserved for adornment of kitchen work-tops!

Discretion should be present when planning this feature of the instrument, and some reference to what is acceptable in some high-class examples may be seen in shops and the hands of other players.

Of course the earlier the original, the less decoration was used, and this is why the ancient examples look plain and simple by comparison with, say the Baroque period, when many instruments were vehicles for the most elaborate of embellishment, frequently to the detriment of its acoustic potential. Then, the probability was that the object would have been commissioned by some wealthy person as a gift to someone who might treasure it highly, but perhaps played it very little, if at all.

Many examples of this type of instrument adorn the walls of galleries and glass cabinets of museums today, having survived because of lack of honest use. The common, inexpensive, instruments belonging to hard working musicians have in most cases been worn out and discarded, leaving few extant examples. The early Spanish guitar known as a vihuela, is a case in point, since only one of its kind is still in existence, and this is almost never revealed to the public, although examination by photograph is enough to indicate that even this could not have been a typical example.

So, great care is advised in deciding what, where, and how the decoration is to be applied. Widths and colours of purfling may vary, so, be sure to order sufficient for the job in hand, with maybe a little to spare, as matching from another batch cannot be guaranteed.

Rosettes, or any circular inlays, whether simple or complex, may be bought ready-made, and suppliers usually have a good selection from which to choose. One of the most valid reasons for acquiring a ready-made rosette, apart from the fact that they are difficult for the inexperienced to produce, is that they will be, or should be, perfectly circular. This is an important feature, if the standard circle cutting tool is used to establish the inner and outer cuts, prior to excavating the required channel.

Caution is necessary with the use of some natural materials used so often for decoration, such as abalone. I understand that the dust given off by abraiding shells of this kind may be carcinogenic, and to spend any length of time crouched over an intricate piece of inlay, scraping, filing, grinding or whatever, had best be done with some protective mask and a liberal draught of fresh air. Other materials may have nasty effects, so beware!

Simple chip-carving techniques may be appropriate to some instruments, particularly the ancient ones with solid members, like the rote, compostelan lute, or psaltery. I recommend the 2-knife methods described so well in the books by Wayne Barton.

Another valid medium for use by the artistically inclined maker is pyrography. Not that I have ever used this myself, but I have seen some beautifully decorated psalteries with pyrographic designs, and no doubt other instruments could be similarly enhanced.

As with any other object, it depends so much on the instrument and how the maker feels about it, as an object to be appraised visually as well as aurally. Appearance plays such an important role in the overall effect that it has to be considered with ultimate care, and in this respect, wise makers will give as much thought to this as in the selection of the appropriate materials used in the construction of the instrument.

11. Action!

The title of this section might well imply the need for prompt activity, or conjure some memory of a wartime predicament in the minds of those with military experience. Most film buffs recognize it as the most galvanic utterance of the director commanding a movie-set. To the luthier, it is none of these things, being one of the more intellectual sections of this book, perhaps even calling for contemplation rather than activity. By the word "action", the player, or maker, means "the height of which the strings are set above the fingerboard". The players of the violin family of instruments rarely, if ever, mention it. One reason for their apparent disinterest in this subject is due no doubt to there being no frets fitted to their instrument although, of course, similar conditions need to be met by the geometry of the string setting associated with the fingerboard. Guitarists on the other hand may well experience spasms of ecstasy when encountering a guitar with some alleged "fantastic" action. Some of the solid, electric, steel-stringed instruments from the U.S.A. or inexpensive Oriental copies, are capable of extracting joyful superlatives complementing this feature as if there were something mystical or unique about it. I must say in passing that those given to the most praise, or criticism, of this particular constituent have been those players who perhaps have displayed the least technique! However, there is little point in upsetting a blissfully ignorant applecart for the sake of scoring easy points. Instead let us look at what "Action" is. Factors involved are as follows:

String tension,

String length,

Height of bridge-saddle,

Height of nut,

Height of frets (where fitted),

Flatness of fingerboard.

Whatever the outcome of the maker's efforts to bring about a satisfactory mix of these ingredients, it may well be viewed as comfortable to one player but not necessarily so to another. In any case we need to know what is required by the player, in terms of his style of playing, and for which type of music. If this sounds rather refined, just hand around a particular instrument to a variety of players and invite their comments on this aspect of it, or listen to the quality of the sound produced. Examining this further we can readily see that we are trying to balance: (a), the need to support the string at a height sufficient to clear the fingerboard during its oscillation, against, (b), the desirability to support it at a height close enough to enable it to be pressed against the fingerboard with the least effort.

To achieve this compromise, assuming that the String tension and String length are correct, and that the fingerboard is flat and true, (more about this later), then we may proceed as follows:

(a) Check the height of the nut;

(b) Check the height of the bridge-saddle;

(c) Check the measurement between the underside of the string and the fingerboard surface halfway along the string. This will be at the twelfth fret if so equipped, and in this case measurements are assumed to be taken from the top of the fret and not from the surface of the fingerboard.

The table of measurements over page represents normal requirements for average conditions of instruments, combined with considerations of types of strings and players.

| Instrument | Millimetres between the underside of the string and the: | |
	first fret or fingerboard at the nut	twelfth fret or fingerboard at mid-point of string
Appalachian Dulcimer	1	3
Mandolin	0.7	2
Mediaeval fiddle	1	4
Compostelan lute	0.5	3
Classic guitar	1	3 on 1st string 4 on 6th string

It is normal to expect to make some adjustment to the above due to minor inconsistencies, (dare we say errors, even?), in the measurements or the construction, so it is as well to be somewhat circumspect in this area.

If an open string buzzes when plucked it may be assumed that the bridge saddle is too low. By "open", it is meant that the string is free to vibrate without being held against the fingerboard. If on the other hand the string buzzes when held against a fretted fingerboard, then the bridge saddle may be raised to eliminate this. Temporary packing may be added under the saddle to achieve this but when a satisfactory adjustment has been reached, a new saddle should be made to avoid any possibility of inefficient transmission of string vibration. There is also the possibility of one or more frets being out of horizontal alignment which may produce a buzz if a string is held at a lower fret. This is a case for patient examination and accepting that the need to spend time removing and replacing strings and carefully adjusting if necessary is a very important part of the job of instrument making. All too often I find well-made instruments which are almost impossible to play because they have been set-up badly. What is worse is that the instrument may find its way to an owner who is not an experienced player, and someone who therefore may not necessarily appreciate that the problems they have in mastering the instrument may not be lack of ability on their part but generated by an incorrect action.

I mentioned more to come about the flat fingerboard. Today we consider that the width of the oscillation of the vibrating string needs a proportionate gap between the string and the fingerboard. Rather obvious, you may say, so therefore one readily appreciates the need for greater clearance for the lower strings than the higher pitched and thinner first string. Also one may assume that the width of oscillation would be greater in the middle of the string than at either end. To compensate for this it is thought by most modern makers to be essential to reduce the thickness of the fingerboard at the end nearest to the bridge, thus creating a greater clearance, without the need to raise the bridge excessively. This calls for experience and a degree of instruction beyond the scope of a book and in any case it is not fundamental to the requirements of the instruments herein.

Nevertheless, the call for accuracy is, as always, paramount and the tenacious craftsman will be rewarded, as Mr W. Shakespeare, of Stratford, put it, "in Action, how like an angel. . ."

12. Fretting Without Tears

Depending on the instrument one needs to consider its frets in terms of "which", "where", and "how". By "which" I mean the type, shape and dimensions of the fret-wire. For most instruments there is generally a small range of sections available, and unless the maker, or the player for whom the instrument is intended, is specific, then use a medium size. It may be possible to sample a similar instrument to check the size of fret, and provided that the measurements are taken with a device made of plastic to avoid possible damage to the instrument, the owner is unlikely to object to the examination.

Most metal frets are of a mushroom or umbrella shape in section, with a tang to fit into a slot cut into the fingerboard. Some early instruments had a simple square-section wire let in to achieve the same result. Bone and ivory have also served the same purpose, but with the obvious disadvantage that, being of a softer material, they wear out in less time than their metal counterparts. Along the sides of the tang on the fret there should be small protruberances shaped like diamonds. These help the fret to grip the sides of the slot sawn into the fingerboard, so, if the fret-wire you are offered does not have this feature, you may prefer to seek a supply elsewhere.

In the case of the softer, tied-on frets, for antique instruments, there is a choice of either gut or nylon. It is not easy to get the latter in a large enough diameter for this purpose with sufficient flexibility to permit its conformation to the shape of the fingerboard with its relatively "tight" corners. It is therefore advisable to use fret gut, and this should be available from string suppliers, or it may be possible to make friends with a violinist or 'cellist and claim their cast-off strings.

The second requirement for satisfactory fretting, regardless of the material, is a knowledge of "where" the frets are to be fitted.

In the "old" days, so I am told, instrument makers used the "Rule of 18". This simply meant that the scale-length, and this is the free vibrating length of the string from nut to bridge, was divided by eighteen, which gave the distance of the first fret from the nut. One then took the distance remaining between the first fret and the bridge and divided by 18 to find the distance from the first fret to the second, and so on. This was hopelessly incorrect, however attractively simple it may seem to be, and I've never yet found an instrument whose frets were fitted to that formulation. Each maker of whom I enquired in my younger days pointed out that the "Rule of 18" was wrong and each smiled with a confidential touch of the nose to imply that I was going to be let into a secret formula before giving me their personal "best".

The numbers, generously given, and gratefully received, all varied from 17.825 to 17.85. When I applied myself to the task of calculating fret positions from these divisors I found that the known positions, these are those at the fifth, seventh, twelfth, and nineteenth frets, giving the degrees of the scale corresponding to the fourth, fifth, twelfth and compound fifth respectively, did not correspond to the fractional analysis which pertained to the positions given by musicologists and theoreticians. In fact, in the case of a scale length of say 600 mm, the musical scale, if it were a perfect world, requires the fifth fret to occur at 450 mm, the seventh at 400 mm, the twelfth at 300 mm and the nineteenth at 200 mm. This was before the days of personal computers, in fact it was before the days of the push-button, give-away-with-petrol, calculators — so, with slide-rule and logarithms, lots of paper and masses of trial and error (mostly error!), I attempted the impossible, because it is impossible to find one number which will divide the scale-length to give these fret positions exactly.

So, we are faced with compromise. Without going into the principles of the tempered scale, or the complications of curvilinear fingerboards, compensations for differing gauges and tensions in strings, etc, etc, I suggest that for all the instruments in this book requiring frets, the following method works satisfactorily, both practically and theoretically:

Take the scale length, i.e. distance from nut to bridge.

Divide this by 1.05945.

The result is the distance from first fret to the bridge.

Divide this by 1.05945.

The result is the distance from second fret to the bridge, and so on, for as many frets as the instruments requires. Please note, you have a progressive checking system if you remember that the following fret positions should coincide with their corresponding fractions of the scale length.

FRET NUMBER	FRACTION OF SCALE LENGTH
5	¾
7	⅔
12	½
19	⅓

We accept that the positions given by the drawing, or, by your own calculations, represent the vibrating lengths of the string. This means that the top of the fret, if it is of the normal rounded shape, should be taken as the point of contact made with the string and from which its length of vibration is measured to the bridge. It may be necessary to emphasize that if the bridge is fitted with a saddle, then its point of contact (with the string) nearest to the fret, is taken as its datum.

Of course, it is easy to get carried away with the project at the pencil and paper stage, but in practical terms, one tenth of a millimeter is as small as most people wish to contend with when faced with the prospect of cutting slots in preparation for fret-fitting!

Which brings us to the question of "how".

Dealing with fret-slots is a question of using the correct width of saw applied at the correct position and cut to the correct depth. There is not much to be gained by measuring the width of the saw since it is the width of the kerf it produces that concerns us. In any case, one needs to test the application practically to be sure of the fit of the fret in the slot. If an off-cut of the fingerboard material is available then a trial run is easy to arrange. If not, then a similar material should be used in order to run an experiment.

Make sure of maintaining the lateral control of the saw by using a marking knife rather than a pencil to establish the fret positions. This will have the advantage of helping to prevent "skidding" of the saw. If two lines are marked with a knife, representing the width of the tang on the fret and also the width of the saw-kerf, then you are doubly sure of the saw control which helps obviate a frayed edge at the top of the slot.

If, as in the case of the guitar, a tapered fingerboard is needed, it is better to mark out the fret on the parallel blank using a set-square to mark the fret positions, before cutting the taper.

Almost without exception it is better to fit the frets to the fingerboard after it has been fitted to the instrument so that final adjustments may be made to make its surface true and straight. The slots are cut after this levelling has been achieved, checking that perfect symmetry and perfect positions are marked before this operation is commenced. That old adage: "mark twice, cut once", was never more applicable! The frets are cut oversize in length and tapped home with a small hammer. As in all hammering operations, it is important to support the member beneath the point at which the hammer is striking. This obviously presents a problem where frets occur over the body of the guitar, so at this point it may be preferred to press home the frets by clamping using the soundhole for access of a G-clamp. It is also advisable to take advantage of today's technology and add a little epoxy resin to the tang when fitting the fret to safeguard its retention in the fingerboard.

Make sure that the fret is closely fitted to, and level across the width of, the fingerboard. The overhang of the oversize fret helps to ensure that the snug fit is carried right to the extreme edge. The excess is trimmed off later when, in fact, all rough edges of fingerboard and frets are smoothed with file and abrasive paper before polishing to make an acceptable finish for the sake of the player's comfort.

After fitting the frets it is necessary to level them to ensure a basis of correct string action (see section with this title). Levelling is readily achieved by rubbing a carborundum stone along the tops of the frets and checking periodically with a straight-edge during the operation. Polishing the tops with a wad of steel wool lubricated with a little linseed oil will burnish both fretting and the fingerboard simultaneously. There are files made especially for the purpose of rounding-off the fret-tops after levelling but as these are expensive and may be used rarely, the wire-wool operation may be thought sufficient.

13. Strings and Fitting Them

It is no longer necessary for the luthier to make his own strings, in fact, most strings can be bought over the counter of well-stocked music stores. Refer to the "List of Suppliers" near the end of this book if you have difficulty in obtaining the strings you need.

Taking the type of string as first consideration, it will be gut, or nylon, steel or bronze. Some strings are made of many strands (multifilament) wound in wire to keep the shape and to add weight whilst maintaining their flexibility.

Here is a chart showing alternatives where appropriate:

INSTRUMENT	MATERIAL	SPECIFICATION
Psaltery	Steel	0.25 mm piano wire
Rote	Steel	Set of low-tension guitar strings
Dulcimer	Steel	2 first and 1 fourth banjo strings
Mandolin	Steel	Standard set for mandolin
Fiddle	Gut or nylon	Standard set for violin
Harp	Gut or nylon	Low-tension (state length with order)
Lute	Gut or nylon	First, second, and fourth, guitar
Guitar	Gut or nylon	Set of low-tension guitar strings

In every case one end of the string is attached by some means to an anchoring device whilst the other end is wound around a tuning pin to adjust the tension.

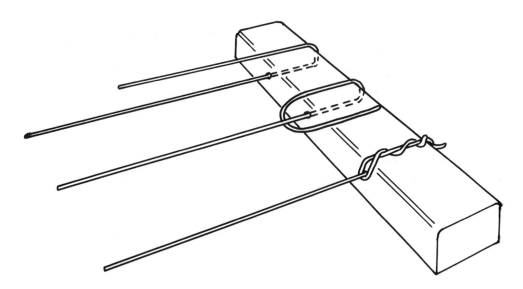

Figure 23   Tying a string on a guitar bridge

Shown below at Fig. 25 is the method of anchoring the fixed end of the string on the psaltery.

Tying on a guitar string often gives problems but this way is effective and secure, provided that the end of the string is tucked under the bend at the bottom of the bridge. This is illustrated in Fig. 23 (page 61).

A string which is attached by a loop is easily provided with one by the simple device shown below. After locating the string in the hook, hold the two ends with pliers and turn the handle at least 10 times. It is easier with two pairs of hands.

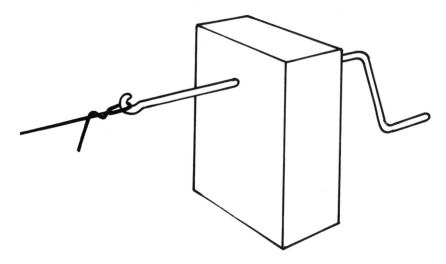

Figure 24   Winding a loop on a string

To attach the string to the tuning peg efficiently and securely to ensure no possibility of slipping, it is necessary to wind at least one turn around the peg to trap the loose end, as shown here for the psaltery, but it applies in principle to all the instruments.

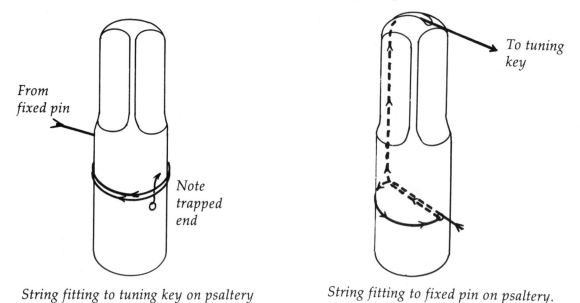

String fitting to tuning key on psaltery

String fitting to fixed pin on psaltery. Note grooved head

Figure 25   Fixing strings to wrest pins

In the case of the harp, the same principle of attachment to the tuning peg applies as to the psaltery and rote, but there is a need to knot the other end of the string to retain it in the soundboard if the pop-rivet system of hole reinforcement is used. See alternative illustration.

*Section through soundboard
showing string-retaining pin*

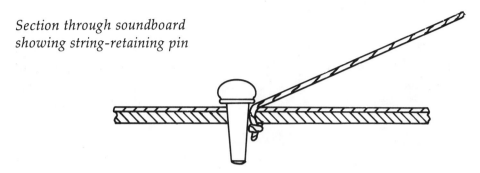

Figure 26   *Alternative string-retaining peg in harp soundboard*

Almost any, and there are many, "authentic" knots for this purpose, and, basically, if the knot is secure and bigger than the hole in the soundboard, then it will suffice. You may like to try this one, which I learned from the Happy Hungerfords.

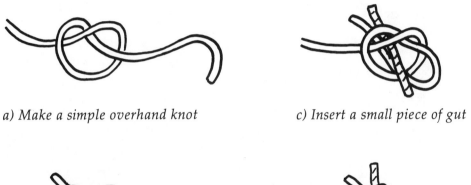

a) Make a simple overhand knot   *c) Insert a small piece of gut*

b) Push the end back through the hole   *d) Pull up the knot tightly*

Figure 27   *Tying a stopper-knot in a harp string*

Tuning lever

For the instruments which use wrest-pins, it is necessary to use a tuning lever of some sort to turn the pins efficiently. On no account use a pair of pliers as this risks slipping and spoiling the square head, effectively ruining the grip for the correct appliance.

Beware when purchasing. I have been sold the wrong lever by the supplier of the wrest-pins! And prices for the same article have varied at different shops by 250%!

Plan Section and Building Guide

14. Bowed Psaltery

CUTTING LIST	PART	QTY	DIMENSIONS (mm)
	A Soundboard	1	3 × 200 × 450
	B Back	1	3 × 200 × 450
	C Long Side	2	20 × 25 × 460
	C Short Side	1	20 × 25 × 200
	D Bridge	1	10 × 10 × 160
	E Tuning Pins	17	5 dia. × 40
	F Fixed Pins	17	5 dia. × 40
	String	–	6 Metres
	Bow	1	5 × 10 × 380

Stage One

Pencil the outline of the psaltery on a stiff board at least 10mm thick.

After preparing the frame to width and thickness, cut to length and decide on the jointing method for the corners. This may be chosen from butt, halved, or mitred joints. The quickest is butt jointing, the most demanding is halved jointing, but I recommend mitring since this is fairly straight-forward and because the joint is not noticed if cut well.

Set up the jointed frame on the building board with glue applied to the joint faces. Place newspaper or tape between the board and the frame where the joints will be located, in order to prevent escaping glue coming into contact with the board. Hammer a few nails into the board on either side of the jointed corners to hold the frame in position whilst the glue is setting. Nothing more elaborate is required in the way of clamping, as the frame is going to be held firm by the soundboard and back of the instrument. When the glue is set, remove the frame from the board and plane both sides of the frame in readiness to receive the soundboard and the back.(See Figures 28 and 29, page 68)

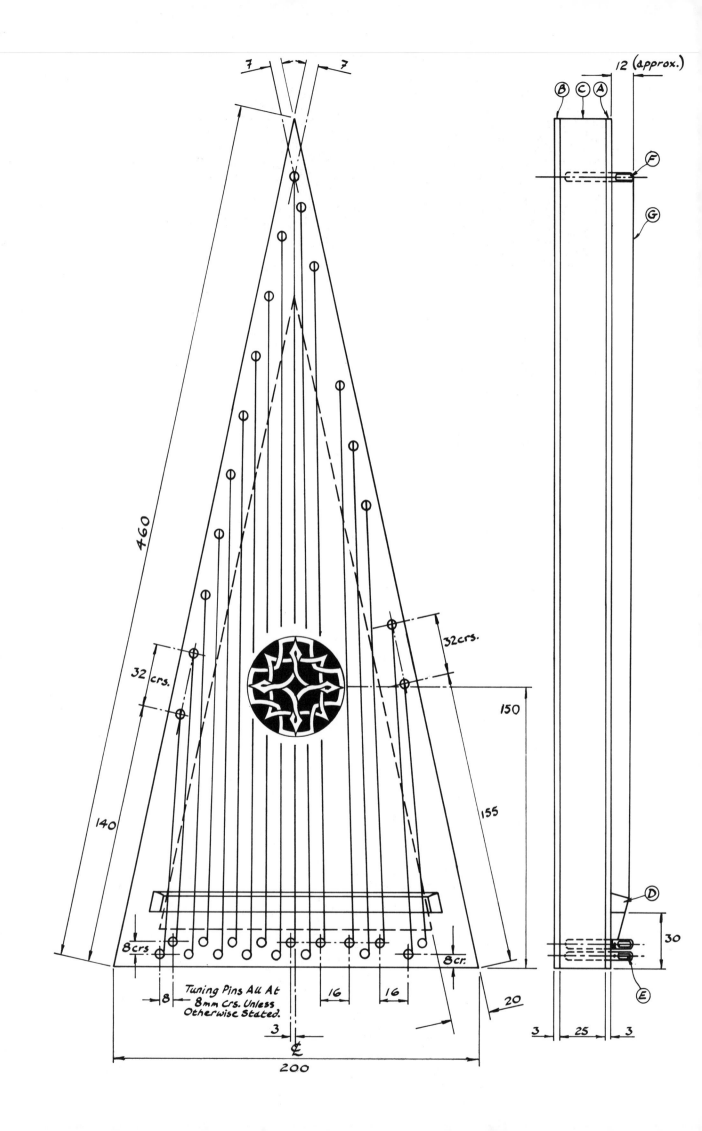

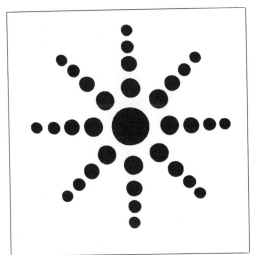

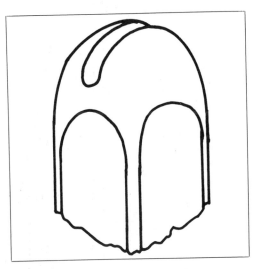

Detail (full size) of 3
alternative rose patterns

Detail of fixed pin F
(not to scale)

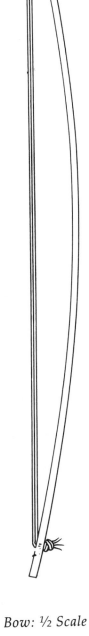

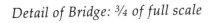
Detail of Bridge: ¾ of full scale

Bow: ½ Scale

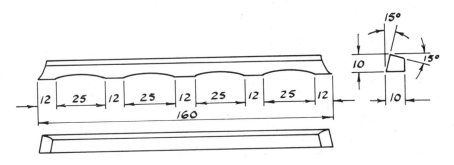

15°

15°

10

10

12 25 12 25 12 25 12 25 12

160

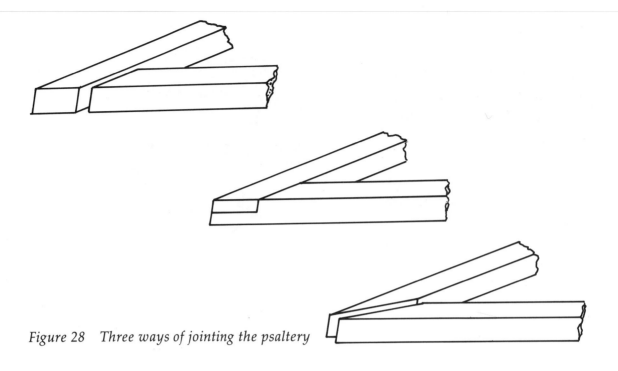

Figure 28   Three ways of jointing the psaltery

Figure 29   Gluing a psaltery on a work board

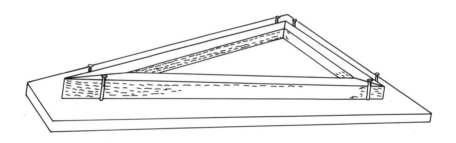

Stage Two

Before fitting the soundboard it is necessary to cut out the soundhole. Choose a style to suit your ability, (even a plain, open hole will suffice, if the maker is a complete beginner), and keep the design to a maximum of 50 mm diameter.

Stage Three

Fix the soundboard and back, simultaneously if you wish, and trim off the excess all round.

Stage Four

Mark the positions of the holes for all the pins, bearing in mind that if you prefer you may put the "white notes" on the left-hand side with "black notes" on the right. Drill the holes with a 3/16" diameter drill which gives just the right "bite" to the 5 mm wrest-pins.

Stage Five

Take off the sharp corners, and chamfer, or round-off, all edges. Finish off according to the instructions in the section on "Finishing".

Stage Six

Take 25 of the 50 wrest-pins and file a groove across their tops in line with the holes which are cross-drilled through the pin shank. Bear in mind that the diameter of the piano wire should be about 0.25 mm which means that a corresponding groove is very shallow. This is to retain the strings on the top of, what we shall now refer to as, the "fixed" pins. Make this groove follow the radius of the crown of the pin in order to bend the string smoothly over its top and without any sharp corners left by the file. The fixed pins are then inserted into the holes located along the two long sides. As will have been noticed, the standard wrest-pin has a fine, multi-start thread from the pointed end up to within a few millimetres of the string-retaining hole. The fixed pins are screwed in as far as the threaded section permits and left with the cross-drilled holes facing in the direction of the tuning pins, that is, in line with the lay of the strings.

Stage Seven

The remaining 25 pins are left ungrooved and fitted into the short side of the psaltery to be used as the "tuning" pins. Now refer to the section "Strings and Fitting Them".

Stage Eight

To make the bow, take a piece of tough, springy hardwood and fashion it as shown in the illustration. Ideal material would be pernambuco, but a piece big enough for a bow would probably cost more than the rest of the materials for the whole instrument! Something such as ash is not only more in keeping, economically speaking, but more appropriate to the instrument as an indigenous tree. It may be necessary to soak it in water overnight before bringing it into contact with gentle heat to prepare it for bending during the string fitting operation.

Stage Nine

The bow-hair, whether of horse-hair or a synthetic equivalent, need be no more than about 30 hairs and is prepared thus: knot one end of the hank and soak it in warm water for a few minutes. Remove from the water, straighten the hank and measure it along the length of the bow. Knot the free end of the hank, without twisting the strands if possible, at a distance slightly less than the distance between the knotches at either end of the bow. One simply bends the bow sufficiently to slip the hank through the knotches and by a little trial and error it is an easy matter to adjust the tension to give a satisfactory arc in the bow. It is prudent to produce this bend over a period of a few days, bringing about the desired bend gradually, by progressively shortening the distance between the knots.

Stage Ten

When dry, the bow-hair may be treated with rosin (not resin, please note) just as one would prepare a conventional violin bow. Holding the block of rosin in one hand one simply draws the bow back and forth across it, pressing the hair firmly and with consistent pressure against the surface of the block to coat it thoroughly. Nothing works as well as horse-hair and even that will not work without rosin.

15. Rote or Lyre

CUTTING LIST	PART	QTY	DIMENSIONS (mm)
	Soundboard	1	4 × 200 × 755
	Back	1	4 × 200 × 755
	Exterior Sides	2	5 × 25 × 710
	Interior Sides	2	5 × 25 × 430
	Bottom Block	1	25 × 25 × 210
	Fork Block	1	25 × 45 × 65
	Bridge	1	10 × 15 × 70
	Peg Block	1	25 × 40 × 200

Stage One

Prepare all internal blocks: peg, fork, bottom, and end blocks.

Stage Two

Draw the outline of the instrument on a building board and attach all blocks temporarily by screws from underneath. Remember to face the board with scrap paper beneath the blocks to prevent excess glue adhering.

Stage Three

Fit the two long (outer) sides and the two short (inner) sides to the blocks and fair off the ends and joints.

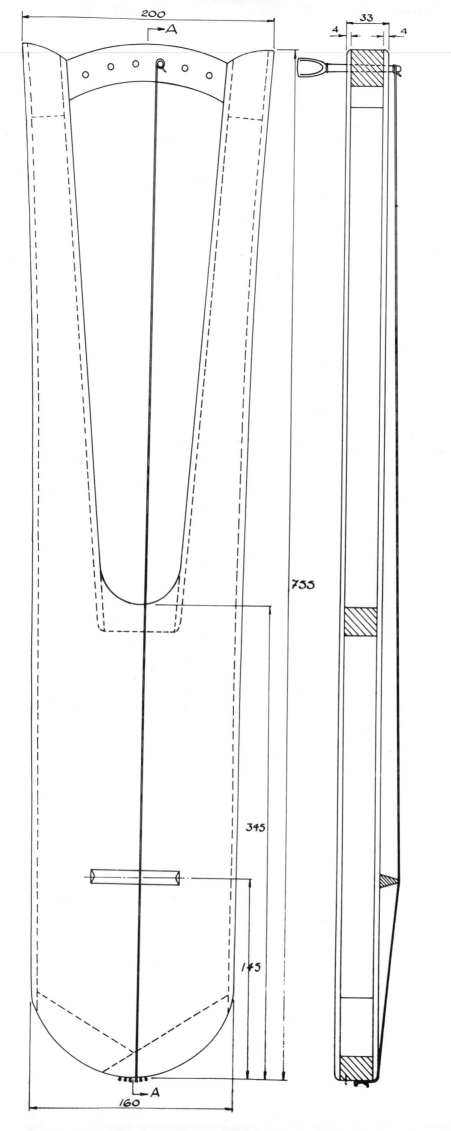

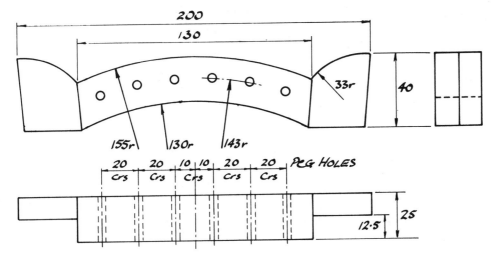

200

130

33r

40

155r   130r   143r

PEG HOLES

20   20   10 10   20   20
Crs   Crs   Crs   Crs   Crs

25

12·5

Peg Block

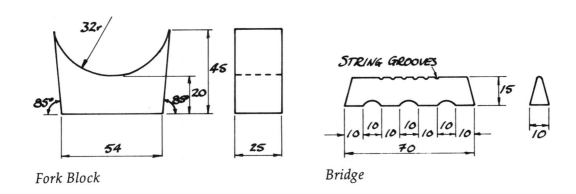

32r

45

20

85°   85°

54

25

STRING GROOVES

15

10 10 10 10 10 10 10

70

10

Fork Block   *Bridge*

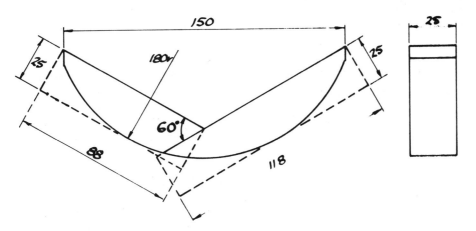

150

180r

25

25

60°

88

118

25

Bottom Block

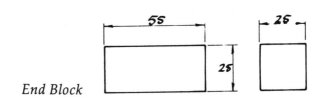

55

25

25

25

End Block

Stage Four

Provided that the upper faces of all the blocks and sides are level and true, the soundboard may be glued on.

Stage Five

Remove the assembly by releasing the screws which held the blocks on the building board and fit the back. When dry, trim all round and chamfer all edges.

Stage Six

Finish the instrument, referring to the section on "Finishing".

Stage Seven

Make the bridge and add the string-retaining nails to the bottom block.

Stage Eight

Fit the tuning pegs. Either steel wrest-pins or wooden pegs may be used, whether made on a lathe or bought from a supplier.

Stage Nine

Refer to the section "Strings and Fitting Them".

16. Compostelan Lute

CUTTING LIST	PART	QTY	DIMENSIONS (mm)
	Body	1	60 × 125 × 465
	Bridge	1	7 × 12 × 50
	Tailpiece	1	5 × 32 × 50

Stage One

As may readily be seen from the plan, this charming little lute is carved entirely from one piece of wood, with the obvious exception of its skin soundboard.

If you are lucky enough to come by a half trunk of a suitable tree, or a complete round which you can divide into two pieces down its length, you already have the basic shape suggested by the natural object. If not, then use a conventional rectangular block. Either way, mark out the outline of the cavity and gouge out the redundant material. Some time may be saved by boring holes prior to gouging.

Stage Two

Cut out the outline of the exterior shape of the instrument with either a band-saw or a bow-saw. Finish off the shaping with spokeshave or draw-knife.

Stage Three

Hollow out the cavity beneath the peg-head and drill the holes for the tuning pegs. These holes must be reamed to match the taper of the pegs, whether made or bought.

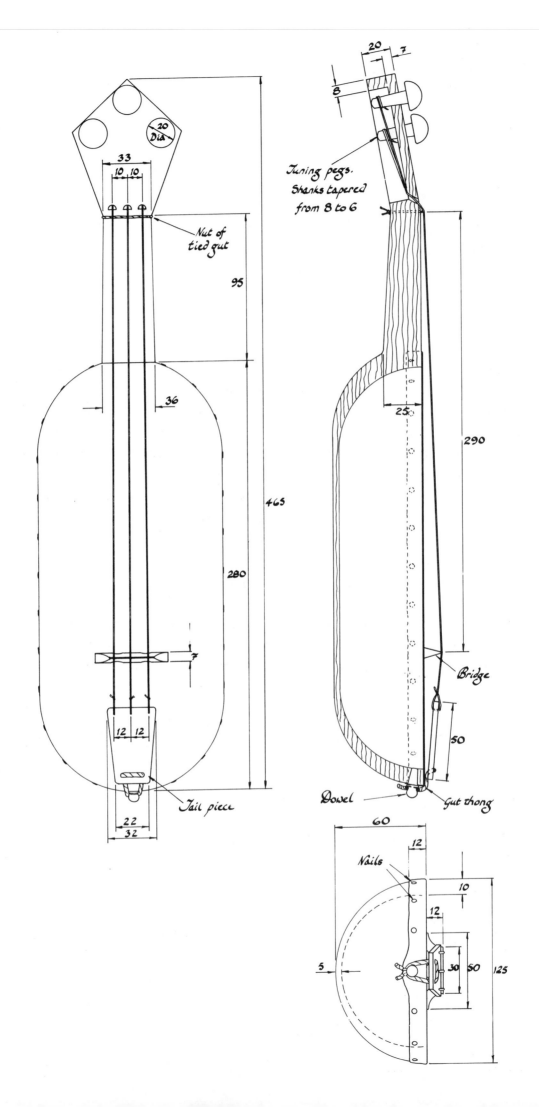

20

7

8

Tuning pegs.
Shanks tapered
from 8 to 6

33

10 10

Nut of
tied gut

95

465

290

36

280

25

Bridge

7

50

12 12

Dowel

Gut thong

Tail piece

22

32

60

12

Nails

10

12

5

30

50

125

Stage Four

Drill the three holes in the peg-head to guide the strings to their respective tuning pegs.

Stage Five

Make the end knob for the thong retention and drill a suitable hole to receive it in the bottom end of the lute.

Stage Six

Acquire the skin, preferably calf or goat, although, if preferred, a modern synthetic will suffice. Soak the membrane in cool water until soft and pliant. Paint the top flat surface and about 10 mm down the side and all round the body where the skin will come into contact. Place the skin on the body whilst it is still damp and stretch it into position with tape or string bound around it. Leave it for 24 hours. Remove the binding and trim off any excess skin leaving a "skirt" of about 12 mm from the top. This should be glued firmly all round and, if you have been careful, with no creases or tucks even at the curved ends.

Stage Seven

Bore pilot holes in the body through the skin at regular intervals and tap in flat headed nails to reinforce the skin-to-body joint. It is possible to retain the skin with nails only, or for that matter with just the glue, but we all know about the reassurance of "belt and braces"!

Stage Eight

Make the bridge and tailpiece. Tie on the latter to the dowel at the bottom of the body. Add the gut "nut" at the head-end of the fingerboard.

Stage Nine

Turn to the sections on "Finishing" and "Strings and Fitting Them" and "Action".

17. Appalachian Dulcimer

CUTTING LIST	PART	QTY	DIMENSIONS (mm)
	Soundboard	1	3 × 132 × 640
	Fingerboard	1	20 × 25 × 805
	Back	1	3 × 132 × 640
	Sides	2	2 × 40 × 700
	Bottom Block	1	25 × 40 × 70
	Top Block	1	25 × 40 × 55
	Fretwire	1	380 mm length

Stage One

Make the fingerboard, complete with frets and tuning gear, although for ease of handling it is best to remove the latter until the construction is complete. Refer to section on "Fretting Without Tears".

Stage Two

Cut out the blocks from a correctly thicknessed piece of softwood and retain the waste for use in clamping later.

Stage Three

Cut out the three formers from 4 or 6 mm plywood.

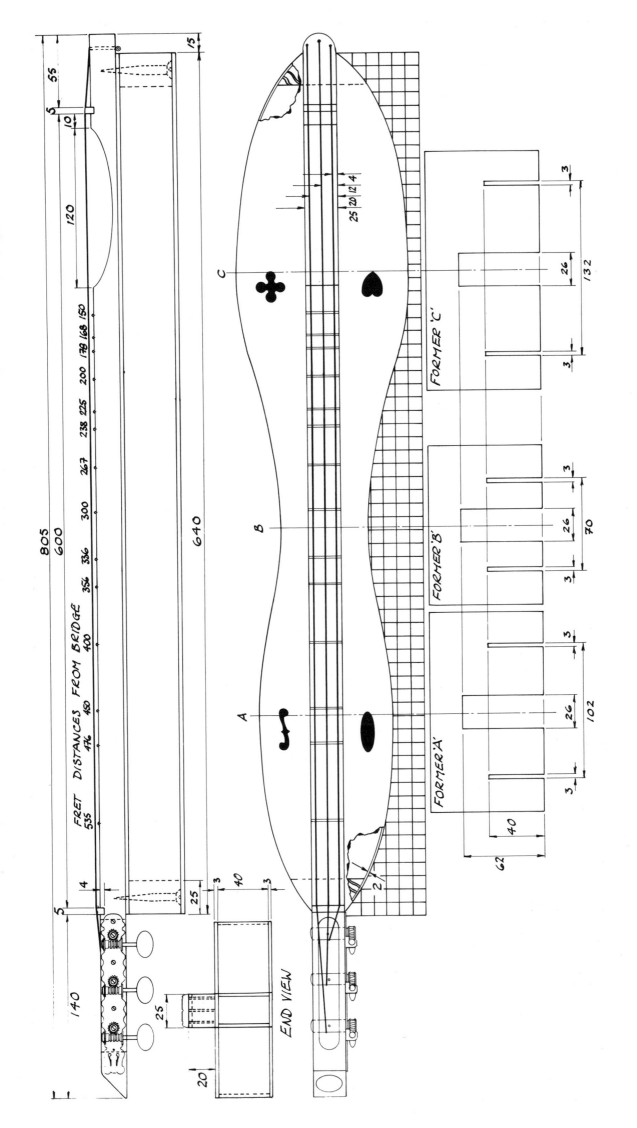

Stage Four

Temporarily fit the blocks to the fingerboard using screws (do not use glue).

Stage Five

Cut the ribs to size leaving some excess in the length. Try a "dry run" (without glue), by making an assembly of the ribs to the blocks using the waste material, as mentioned earlier, to assist with the clamping (Fig. 30). Fit the formers to create the shape of the soundbox. If necessary, warm the ribs to help them conform to the shape imposed by the formers. In the case of a stubborn material, apply direct heat with a bending iron. (See section "Some Devices to Make"). Glue the ribs to the blocks when the shape is correct and length adjusted.

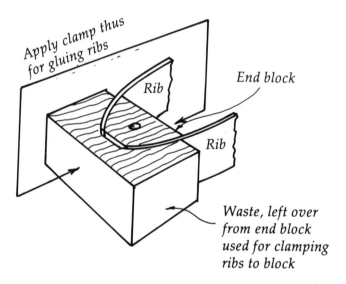

Figure 30   Clamping the dulcimer ribs to the end blocks

Stage Six

Remove the screws from the soundbox/fingerboard assembly and slide out the fingerboard, leaving the formers in position to retain the shape of the soundbox. If need be, temporarily attach a piece of scrap wood to the top of the blocks to hold them apart at the prescribed distance, to ensure a compatible re-marriage with the fingerboard later.

Stage Seven

Prepare the bottom and fit it to the ribs.

Stage Eight

Prepare the soundboard and fit and glue it to the fingerboard.

Stage Nine

Assemble the two modules to complete the instrument and trim all round.

Stage Ten

Refer to sections on Finishing, Action and Strings.

18. Flat-backed Mandolin

CUTTING LIST	PART	QTY	DIMENSIONS (mm)
	Soundboard	1	2 × 185 × 304
	Neck	1	44 × 45 × 300
	Fingerboard	1	3 × 50 × 235
	Back	1	2 × 185 × 304
	Sides	2	2 × 46 × 370
	Bottom Block	1	10 × 40 × 46
	Braces	1	6 × 10 × 770
	Linings	4	3 × 7 × 335
	Bridge	1	5 × 8 × 110
	Fretwire	1	850 mm length
	Headfacing	1	2 × 60 × 147

Stage One

Make the neck completely, including the preparation of the head for the tuning gear, but do not fit the latter as yet.

Stage Two

Prepare the bottom block.

Stage Three

Draw the outline of the finished mandolin on a building board, and fit the neck and block to their respective locations bottom-side uppermost.

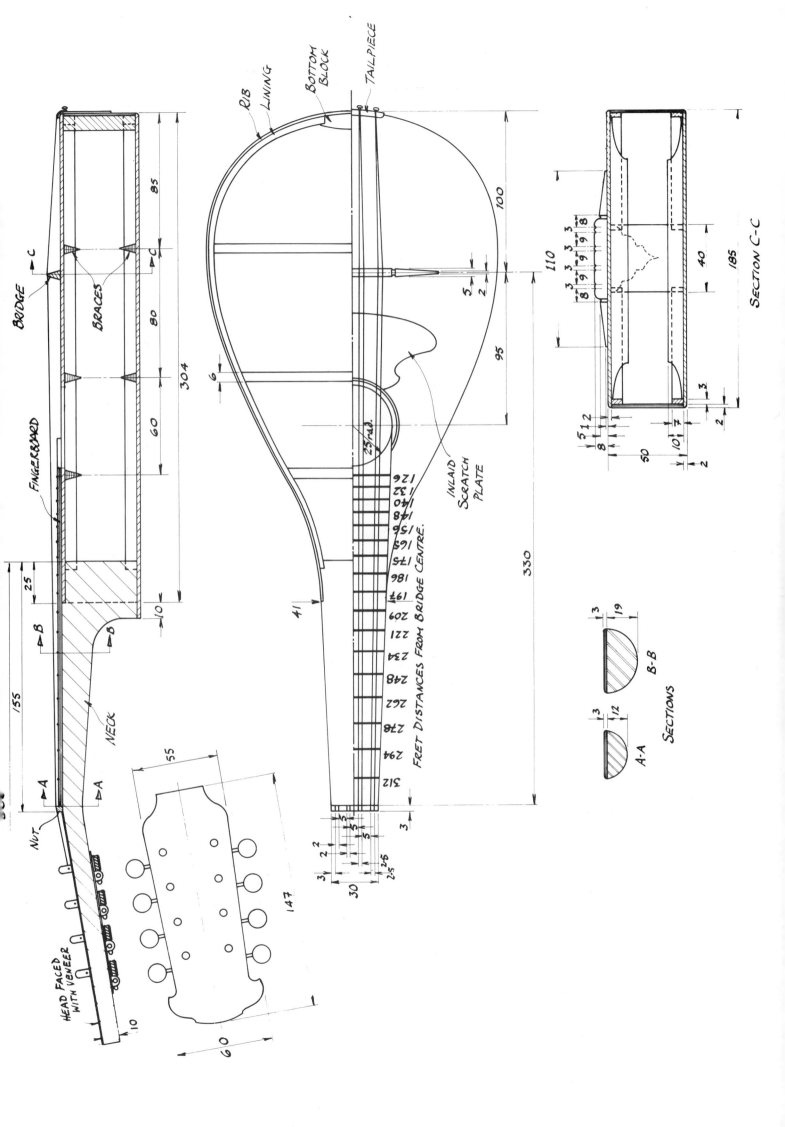

Stage Four

Make the ribs and bend them to shape on a bending iron. The ribs may be a pair or made from one piece.

Stage Five

Fit the ribs to the block and neck. Experiment without glue to ascertain correct fitting of the ribs to the neck and to verify their correct length. Remember to put paper between the components and the building board to avoid contact with excess glue.

Stage Six

Prepare and fit linings around the top and bottom of the ribs, making sure that they are trimmed flush to receive the soundboard and back respectively.

Stage Seven

Make the soundboard and cut the soundhole. Inlay a rosette or other decoration at this stage, plus the scratch-plate if one is to be fitted. The latter may be fitted flush with the surface of the soundboard or stuck on top if desired. Fit braces to the soundboard and glue to the ribs and linings. Trim all round when dry.

Stage Eight

Prepare the back and fit the braces. When dry, glue to the ribs and linings.

Stage Nine

Make the fingerboard with reference to the section on "Fretting Without Tears".

Stage Ten

Fit the tailpiece.

Stage Eleven

Finish off with careful study of sections dealing with Finishing, Action and Strings.

Note: Since completing the main text of this book, I have conducted experiments with this mandolin with the addition of a sound-post. This may surprise some readers, but it was done for several reasons. One was to see if the soundpost improved tone and/or volume by transmitting vibrations to the back-plate, and two, to help support the soundboard, which has a tendency to "dip" in time due to the downwards pressure of the strings on the bridge, as do all flat-topped instruments.

Of course, a fundamental reason for not including a soundpost ordinarily to this type of instrument, is that its back is held against the body of the player, effectively damping-out most of its potential to respond sympathetically anyway. Unlike the violin family, which uses a sound-post effectively because its back is free to vibrate since no contact is made with the player apart from its extreme end and the neck.

My experiments showed that there was a slight increase in volume though little discernible change in the tone, and there seems little doubt that the structural support imparted to the soundboard would help to keep it flat. Some further trials are necessary to ascertain exactly where the sound-post should be placed for the most efficient result.

To fit a sound-post is readily accomplished as follows:

Cut a sound-post from some straight-grained spruce or similar. It should be round in section like a dowel, 4 or 5 mm diameter should be sufficient, and say, ¼ mm to ½ mm longer than the internal distance from the soundboard to the back of the instrument. This may be measured through the soundhole. The easiest method of fixing is to beg, or borrow a sound-post setter, or get a friendly violinist to fit it for you. As to placing it, I suggest you try it in the middle of the inlaid scratch-plate, making sure it is perpendicular to the top and bottom as you fit it. Only the contact and the pressure on the slightly oversize sound-post maintains its location, no glue should be used to retain it.

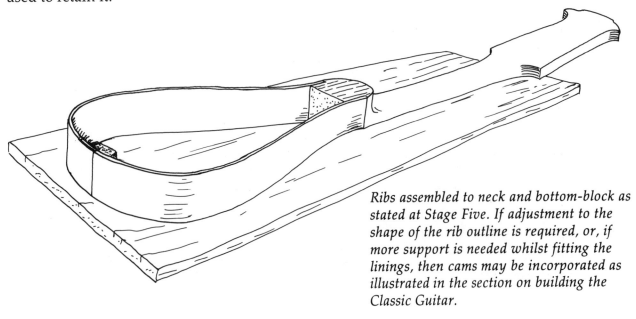

Ribs assembled to neck and bottom-block as stated at Stage Five. If adjustment to the shape of the rib outline is required, or, if more support is needed whilst fitting the linings, then cams may be incorporated as illustrated in the section on building the Classic Guitar.

19. Mediaeval Fiddle

CUTTING LIST	PART	QTY	DIMENSIONS (mm)
	Soundboard	1	3 × 200 × 358
	Neck	1	45 × 48 × 230
	Fingerboard	1	7 × 45 × 150
	Back	1	2 × 200 × 350
	Ribs	4	1.5 × 45 × 215
	Bottom Block	1	25 dia. × 45
	Waist Block	2	40 dia. × 45
	Linings	8	3 × 8 × 215
	Bridge	1	10 × 15 × 60
	Head Facing	1	2 × 90 × 100
	Tailpiece	1	5 × 40 × 80
	Bow	1	5 × 10 × 380

Stage One

Draw the outline of the fiddle on a building board. Make the neck, waist blocks and bottom block and fit them, topside down, onto the building board, attached temporarily by screws from underneath.

Stage Two

Prepare a quartet of ribs, over-long, for trimming later. Bend them with the bending iron, with reference to the section "Tricks of the Trade". Check and trim to length and fit all four ribs into appropriate slots in corresponding blocks.

Stage Three

Cut the linings to size, bend to shape with the bending iron and glue into place on the ribs. Trim flat and level to receive the soundboard and bottom.

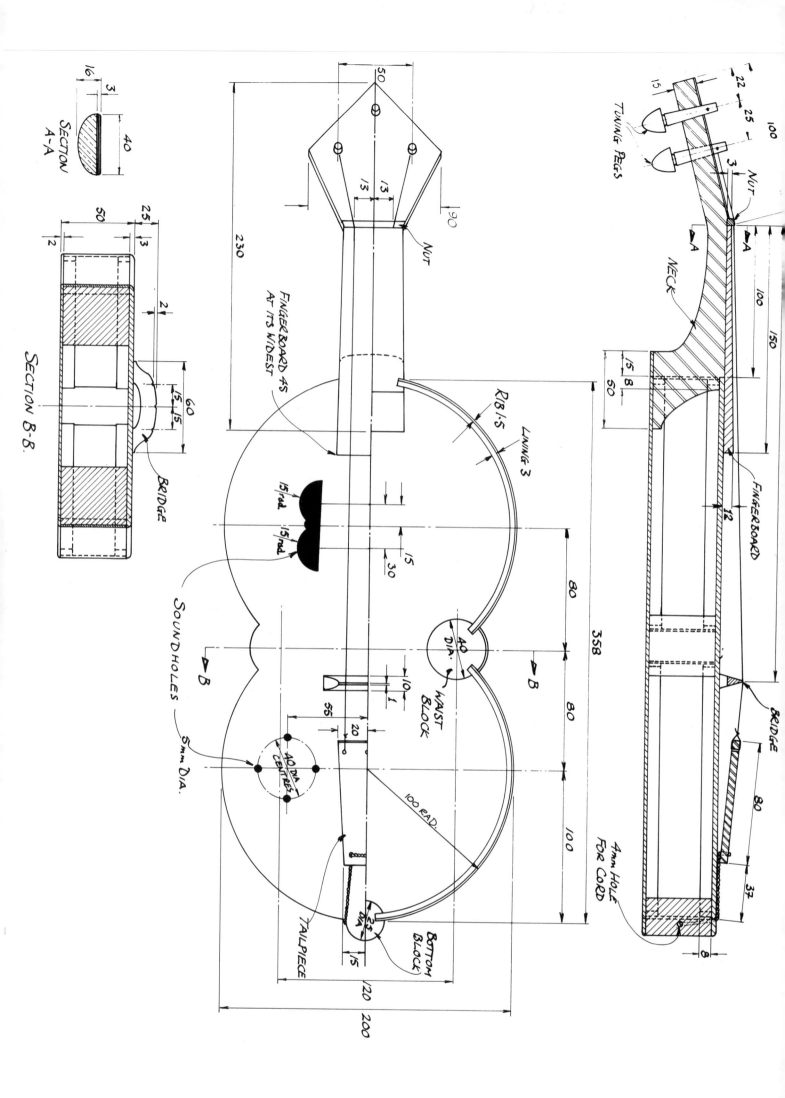

SECTION A-A

16 · 3 · 40

SECTION B-B.

50 · 25 · 2 · 3 · 2 · 15 · 15 · 60

BRIDGE

TUNING PEGS

15 · 22 · 25 · 100 · 3

NUT

NECK

A · A

15 · 8 · 50

100 · 150

FINGERBOARD

12

BRIDGE

4mm HOLE FOR CORD

80 · 37 · 8

50

13 · 13 · 13

90

230

NUT

FINGERBOARD 45 AT ITS WIDEST

RIB 1·5

LINING 3

15/rad.

15/rad.

SOUNDHOLES

5mm DIA.

40 DIA CENTRES

30 · 15

40 DIA.

WAIST BLOCK

80 · 80 · 100

358

B · B

TAILPIECE

100 RAD.

25 DIA.

BOTTOM BLOCK

55 · 20 · 10 · 1

15 · 120 · 200

Stage Four

Fit and glue the soundboard.

Stage Five

Fit and glue the bottom.

Stage Six

Make and fit the fingerboard.

Stage Seven

Make and fit the head-facing. This is a decorative veneer or lamination of several veneers not less than 1 mm, not more than 2 mm. Its multi-function includes that of retaining the "nut" (string-rest), at the top of the fingerboard. In other words, the gap left between the head-facing and the fingerboard must be just sufficient to receive the nut and hold it securely without wobbling, as this is not glued.

Stage Eight

Make the tailpiece and attach it to the bottom block with a gut or nylon cord of adequate strength to hold the tailpiece against the pull of the three strings.

Stage Nine

Make the nut and bridge. Remember the string-grooves should be no deeper than half the depth of the strings. Refer to the section "Strings and Fitting Them".

Stage Ten

Make or acquire the tuning pegs and fit the strings.

Stage Eleven

Make the bow as detailed in the chapter on the bowed psaltery.

20. Gothic Harp

CUTTING LIST	PART	QTY	DIMENSIONS (mm)
	Soundboard	1	15 × 120 × 710
	Neck	1	40 × 170 × 322
	Back	1	25 × 120 × 710
	Foot	1	25 × 60 × 70
	Pillar	1	40 × 85 × 795
	Tuning Pins	21	5 dia. × 40

Stage One

Identify the parts on the plan over page: Pillar, Head, Foot, Soundboard, and Body.

Draw the outlines of the pillar and head on to the chosen raw pieces and make the parts. It is best to produce first the mortise and tenon which connect the two members. If the concave corner mouldings prove too elaborate for your present skills, then a 45 degree chamfer is acceptable. Drill the 3/16″ holes for the 5 mm tuning pins.

Stage Two

Mark the shapes of the two parts on the selected pieces for the soundboard and body, plane true and level the faces to be joined.

Stage Three

Carve the interior shape of the soundboard using a cardboard template at each end to verify the internal shape.

Stage Four

Carve the outer shape of the soundboard remembering that the narrow end must blend with the pillar at the joint. Do not try to get a perfect fit at this stage but leave a little excess to be faired-off later.

Stage Five

Fit the backing strip to the underside of the soundboard. This is made from a hard wood or, better, Formica, or similar laminate, and it is glued into place to reinforce the soundboard against the string pull.

Stage Six

Mark out the string positions and drill the holes of sufficient diameter to receive either the pop-rivets, or the alternative string-retaining pins. The former make excellent hole-reinforcements and enhance the soundboard if polished. The latter will appeal to those with a lathe and a liking for repetitive turning. (See Fig. 26 in the section "Strings and Fitting Them").

Stage Seven

Carve the body shape, inside and out. I prefer to do this in that order since the block will stand firm if the interior is carved first and the flat surface to be joined to the soundboard will also lie flat on the bench whilst the outer form is carved. Much of the latter work may be produced with plane, spokeshave, or draw-knife.

Stage Eight

Mark out and cut the three long holes in the back of the body. These are to give access for string fitting.

Stage Nine

Joint the faces of the soundboard to the body ensuring a close fit all round and glue together.

Stage Ten

Make the mortise and tenon at the head/body joint but do not glue as yet.

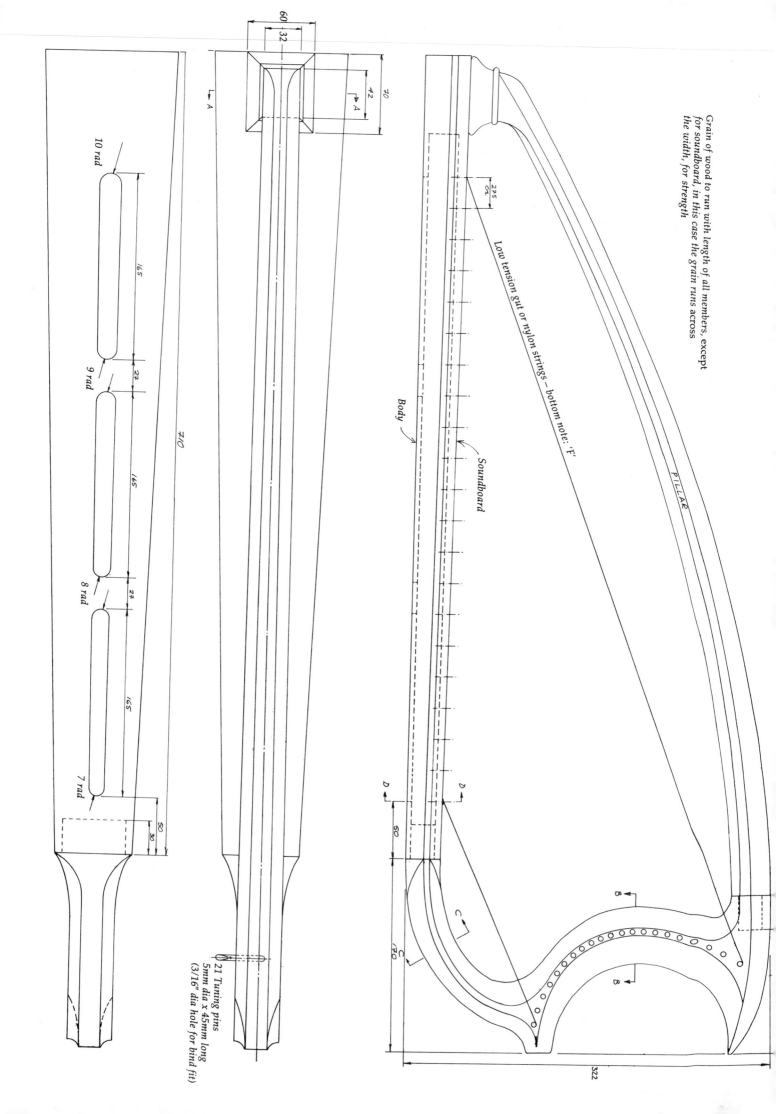

Grain of wood to run with length of all members, except for soundboard, in this case the grain runs across the width, for strength

PILLAR

Low tension gut or nylon strings — bottom note: 'F'

Body

Soundboard

21 Tuning pins
5mm dia x 45mm long
(3/16" dia hole for bind fit)

10 rad

9 rad

8 rad

7 rad

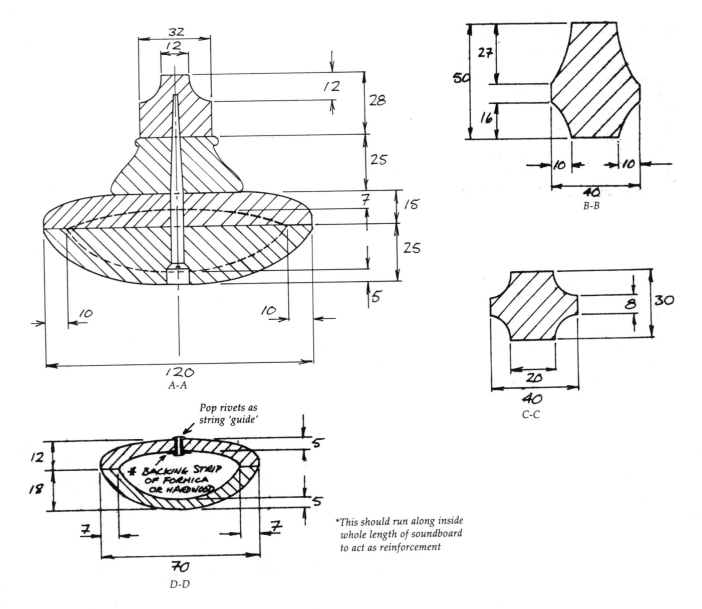

32
12
12
28
25
7
15
25
5
10
10
120
A-A

27
50
16
10
10
40
B-B

8
30
20
40
C-C

Pop rivets as
string 'guide'

12
18
BACKING STRIP
OF FORMICA
OR HARDWOOD

5
5
7
7
70
D-D

*This should run along inside
whole length of soundboard
to act as reinforcement

Stage Eleven

Fit the head to the body and make the foot to connect the bottom of the pillar to the body.

Stage Twelve

Drill a hole for the foot joint, and assemble and glue the foot/body/pillar joint and the mortise and tenon at the head/body joint.

Stage Thirteen

Complete the instrument with reference to the sections for "Finishing" and "Strings and Fitting Them".

21. Classic Guitar

CUTTING LIST	PART	QTY	DIMENSIONS (mm)
	Soundboard	1	3 × 295 × 450
	Neck	1	20 × 75 × 800
	Fingerboard	1	3 × 60 × 425
	Back	1	2 × 295 × 450
	Sides	2	1.5 × 85 × 630
	Bottom Block	1	15 × 50 × 85
	Bridge	1	8 × 27 × 170
	Saddle	1	2.5 × 10 × 75
	Nut	1	5 × 10 × 52
	Fretwire	1	1250 mm length
	Head Facing Outer	1	2 × 75 × 170

Stage One

Prepare a blank for the neck, planed square and true, of overall dimensions 800 × 75 × 20 mm. Cut it and glue the pieces together according to the arrangement as shown in the illustration. Fit the head-facing to tidy up the head and to hold the nut in position as the latter is not glued. Adjustment of the action is facilitated if the nut is readily removable. Complete the shaping of the neck and prepare the head to receive the tuning machines but do not fit these until the instrument is completed.

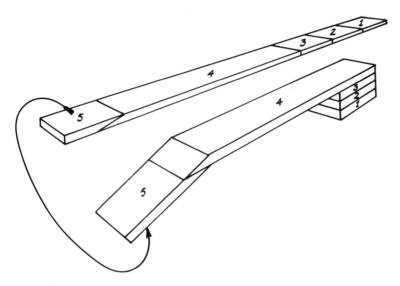

Figure 31   Making up a neck assembly for the guitar

Stage Two

Make the bottom block.

Stage Three

Prepare a building board with an outline of the guitar drawn accurately upon it, including a centre line for symmetrical control. Make cylindrical cams on a lathe, or cut them from dowel stock of between 40 and 50 mm. Alternatively, produce them as per the one illustrated made from a piece of square section stock. Whichever style of cam suits you, it nevertheless requires the screwhole to be drilled off-centre, or it will not act as a cam. The same illustration shows an arrangement using the cams to support the ribs and hold them in the bent position whilst gluing or during the constructional work. (Fig. 32)

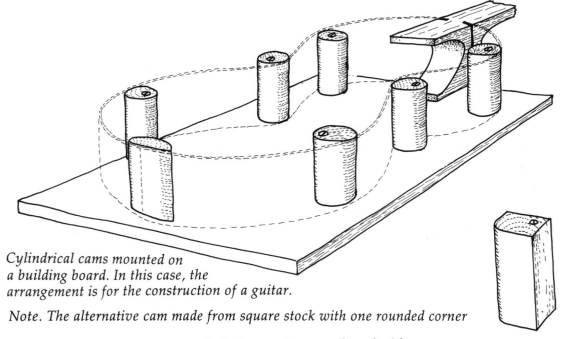

*Cylindrical cams mounted on
a building board. In this case, the
arrangement is for the construction of a guitar.*

Note. The alternative cam made from square stock with one rounded corner

Figure 32   Building a guitar on a board with cams

Stage Four

Turn the neck upside down and attach it to the building board with screws from underneath. Similarly, fix the bottom block, in readiness for Stage Six.

Stage Five

Prepare the ribs and bend them to the required shape with reference to the section "Tricks of the Trade".

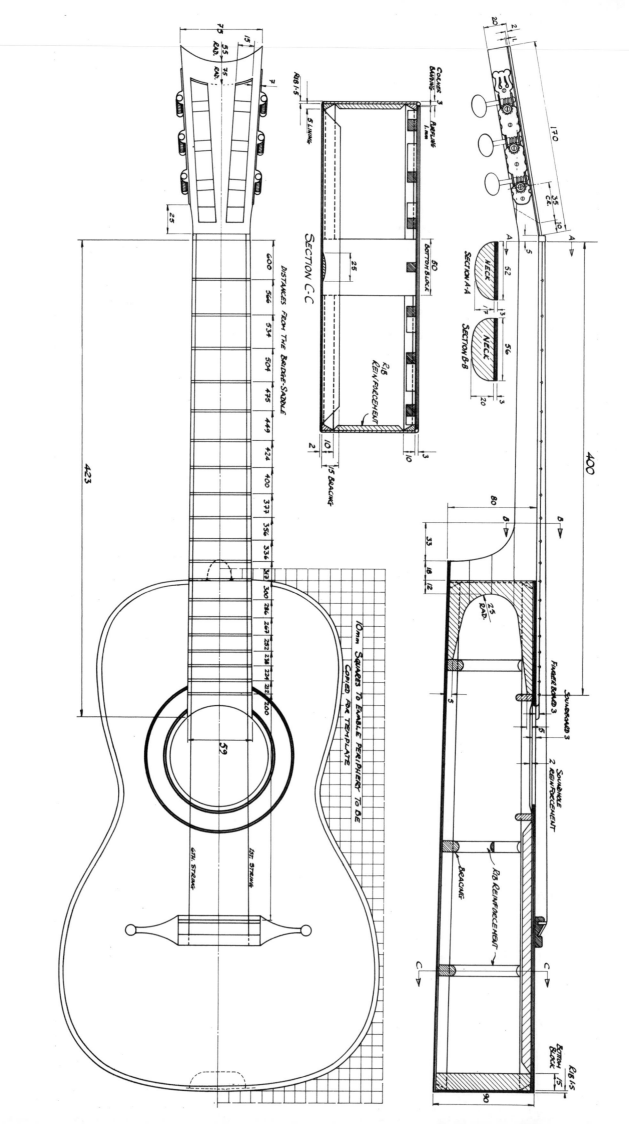

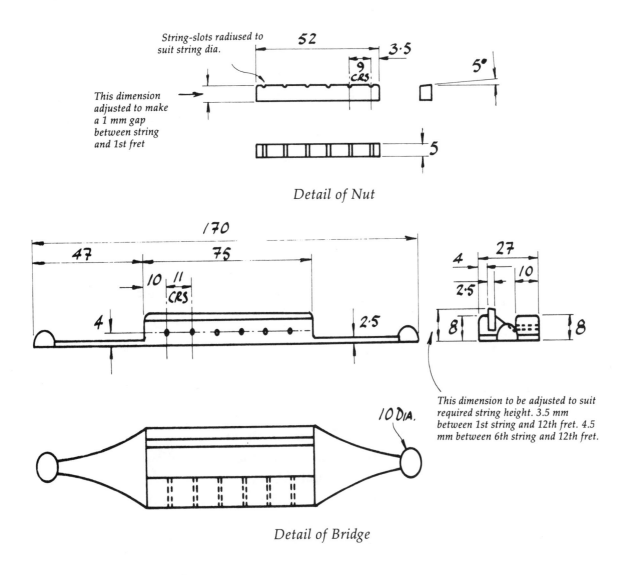

Detail of Nut

Detail of Bridge

This dimension to be adjusted to suit required string height. 3.5 mm between 1st string and 12th fret. 4.5 mm between 6th string and 12th fret.

Stage Six

Check with a dry run to see that the grooves in the neck, prepared for the ribs, are correct in width and depth and glue them into position. Do not glue them to the bottom block until the neck joint is dry, then trim to length to ensure their meeting together in the centre of the bottom block and glue them to the block. Throughout the procedure, the cams are used to maintain the shape of the ribs.

Stage Seven

Note the taper in the body depth and reduce the height at the neck joint according to the plan. Adjust this carefully checking with a flat board placed occasionally on the ribs to ensure their flatness.

Stage Eight

Add the linings to the top and bottom of the ribs and flush them off level with the rib face to receive the soundboard and back. The rib reinforcement may be added at this time. When dry, the structure should be rigid enough to handle without the cams or the building board. However it is reassuring to use the support given by these devices so they may be used for some time yet to advantage.

Stage Nine

Prepare the soundboard by centre-jointing the book-matched pair of pieces with reference to the section "Tricks of the Trade".

Stage Ten

Make the rosette. It is my suggestion for this model to cut and inlay a circle of rosewood or ebony from a veneer, with a double purfling on the inner and outer edges. If done well it can appear very striking and tasteful. Machine cut rosettes are produced to a very high standard and these can be bought relatively cheaply if something more sophisticated is preferred. Use a single blade circle cutter and a hand router (or "old-woman's-tooth", as it used to be called) to prepare the bed for the inlay.

Stage Eleven

Cut the soundhole, after fitting the rosette, and proceed with the fitting of the bracing and fan-strutting of the soundboard.

Stage Twelve

Fit the soundboard, making certain that the struts and braces do not foul the linings so preventing a flush fitting of the ribs to the soundboard. Adhesive tape and elastic bands are useful at this stage. Trim off excess soundboard to bring level with the ribs.

The drawing of the guitar herein, shows a typical flat-topped and flat-bottomed instrument. For makers who prefer to arch either or both of these members, it is readily achieved by shaping the cross bracing to the required arch, say a 2 mm to 4 mm rise in

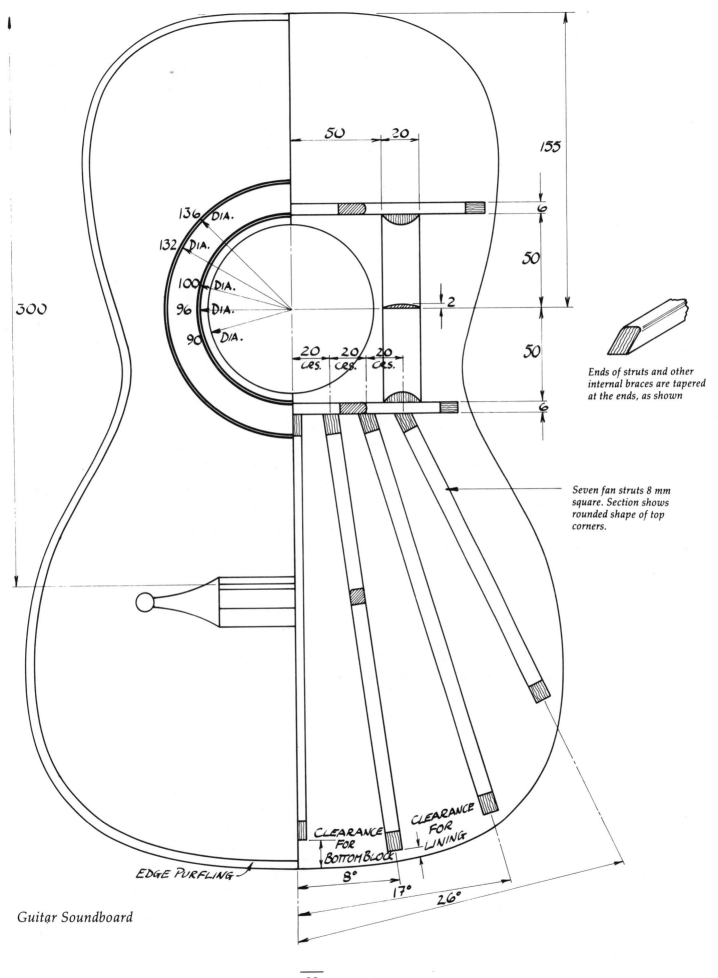

50
20
155
136 DIA.
132 DIA.
100 DIA.
96 DIA.
90 DIA.
300
6
50
2
50
20 CRS.
20 CRS.
20 CRS.
6

Ends of struts and other internal braces are tapered at the ends, as shown

Seven fan struts 8 mm square. Section shows rounded shape of top corners.

EDGE PURFLING

CLEARANCE FOR BOTTOM BLOCK
CLEARANCE FOR LINING

8°
17°
26°

Guitar Soundboard

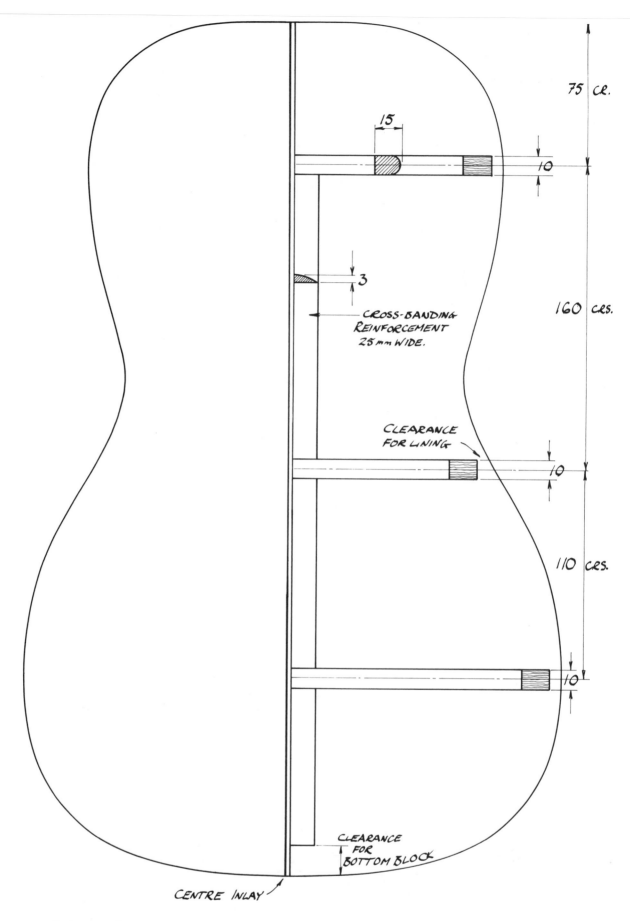

75 CRS.

15

10

3

CROSS-BANDING
REINFORCEMENT
25 mm WIDE.

160 CRS.

CLEARANCE
FOR LINING

10

110 CRS.

10

CLEARANCE
FOR
BOTTOM BLOCK

CENTRE INLAY

Guitar Back

the centre of the boards. When they are glued into position it should result in curving the boards accordingly.

It is better to arrange the arched braces on a flat surface, with curve upwards, and, prior to gluing, lay the prepared board on top, allowing time for it to "fall" into the desired shape, to obviate strain in the gluing process.

It follows that such an arch raises the height of the soundboard, which means that either the height of the bridge, or the thickness of the fingerboard must be adjusted to compensate for this, in order to keep the string action correct.

Stage Thirteen

If corner purfling is to be added it is best done now. A satisfactory rebating tool of the marking-gauge type is best for the preparation of the rebate. An enormous choice of purfling is available from cabinetmaker's suppliers and the like, but it may well be referred to as banding or stringing. Call it what you will, it does the same job of decorating and protecting the corners of the guitar.

Stage Fourteen

Make and fit the braces and cross-banding reinforcement to the back. Remove the body structure from the building board and fit the back. Trim when the glue is dry.

Stage Fifteen

Make and fit the fingerboard. I prefer to fit the frets after the fingerboard is fitted in order that it may then be planed true and level on the neck. Mark the fret positions with a knife to "hold" the saw to ensure accuracy. Make certain that the saw blade is correct for the job. Cut a gap big enough to admit the tang of the fret with a tap from a light hammer, but tight enough to hold it securely. A smear of epoxy on the tang will help to allay fears. Do smooth off the edges of the frets carefully. Check for fine points of fret-fitting in the section "Fretting Without Tears".

Stage Sixteen

Make the bridge, leaving the height of the saddle somewhat high for adjustment later. The saddle, ideally made from ivory or bone, should never be glued in position as the string-pressure retains it anyway and removal may be necessary to adjust the action from time to time.

Stage Seventeen

Mark the position of the bridge and tape around its location to help prevent its movement during gluing. Bear in mind that the scale length of 600 mm is measured from the edge of the nut nearest the bridge to the edge of the saddle nearest the nut. I know that may sound like a conundrum, but it simply means the length of the vibrating string. Use bridge clamps of sufficient length to reach through the soundhole for this operation.

Stage Eighteen

Finish the instrument with reference to the section "Finishing".

Stage Nineteen

Make and fit the nut, tuning machines, saddle and strings. Read the section dealing with the "action" and "stringing" for help with this.

22. Choosing Music for the Instruments

Musical instruments generally fall into one of three categories. To quote the late Benjamin Britten, you either "bow it, blow it, or bang it". And whilst this divides them technically we have to consider their musical characteristics to determine the kind of music best suited to them. Another categorization might be to divide into "monodic" (one-voiced, like a trumpet, for example), or "polyphonic" (many-voiced, such as a piano). We may further divide instruments into their role-category, such as those which play melody, those which play accompaniment, and those which can play both simultaneously. Here is a chart to help to see them graphically.

	MELODY	ACCOMPANIMENT	BOTH
Psaltery	*		
Rote		*	
Dulcimer	*	*	*
Mandolin	*		
Fiddle	*		
Harp	*	*	*
Lute	*	*	*
Guitar	*	*	*

It must be stressed that in cases such as the psaltery, fiddle and mandolin whilst more usually associated with playing tunes, if in the company of other instruments they may well be required to play a descant, or supporting role as part of an accompaniment. In the case of the dulcimer and lute, they "accompany" themselves by producing a drone effect on lower pitched strings in support of the melody on the high "chanterelle" string, in the same manner as bagpipes. There is also the question of selecting music suggested by the nature of the instrument in terms of its ethnic origins, or in the case of a multi-national variety such as the harp, the music suggested by a particular era. One accepts a need for many musicians, particularly beginners, to copy some performer-idol, or some special rendering which has pleased or inspired them. In this respect I am not the "purist" that many might suspect, and although I would not think an arrangement of Handel's "Messiah" for banjo and bassoon a very wholesome idea, such reactions usually stem from nostalgic, emotional, or traditional prejudice. Either way, a beginner is unlikely to do a great deal of harm if some experimentation is undertaken, and it is after all, a fairly basic urge which prompts one to express oneself in music, and should as far as possible, be a creative art. Assuming the student is wise enough to acquire lessons from a qualified tutor to obtain best results from the instrument and themselves, then the choice of music grows in proportion to one's facility.

Here are some suggestions based on my own experience, which I hope will get you off in the right direction, rather than limit your musical boundaries:

Bowed Psaltery   Try it in groups of three playing from music arranged for recorder trios.

Rote   Looks good in classic drama productions and is effective as accompaniment to a song or narrative.

Appalachian Dulcimer   Although this is known throughout Europe in one form or another, as its name suggests this type is associated with folk tunes of the Appalachian Mountains. Much of this is based on British folk music anyway, so it is a wide choice.

Flat-backed Mandolin   The traditional Neapolitan ballads, oozing with romance or tragedy, are the most obvious choice for this charming instrument, but it is a regular visitor to the folk club as well as the classical concert. Vivaldi was only one of the latter-day composers to treat it seriously.

Mediaeval Fiddle   Since this is an instrument of the Middle Ages one is more inclined to use it for formal music in an ecclesiastic setting. It is also perfectly satisfactory in the company of folk bands.

Gothic Harp   Early ballads and sacred songs accompanied by this elegant instrument are very effective, but it is equally pleasing when used for traditional tunes as a solo instrument.

Compostelan Lute   This quaint little instrument is best used providing a percussive drone accompaniment to dance tunes or simple songs. Although somewhat limited in range it is amusing to play tunes on the first string, with rhythmic accompaniment on the lower ones, rather after the fashion of the Appalachian dulcimer.

Classic Guitar   Of all the instruments in this list, this is likely to be the one most popular, and with its facility to play melody and accompaniment in the most complex fashion, the choice of music is endless. Despite the "classic" designation, the term applies more correctly to the general style of the instrument and the manner of its technique, rather than some chronological limitation to its repertoire. In fact, many concerts given by contemporary performers may contain music from the Baroque to the present day with examples from all styles in between.

Naturally, as with all instruments, each has its individual limitations which is another good reason to associate them with others of a different character. In this book there is the potential for ensembles of many varieties, such as:

Fiddle, psaltery, rote, harp, and lute	For Early music
Mandolin and harp	For Classical or Baroque
Mandolin and guitar	For Classical or Baroque
Fiddle, dulcimer, mandolin	For Folk music

And so I leave you with a wide choice of instruments and music. I hope you have been able to use some of my experience to reduce your own trials and errors. If my ideas and techniques have been of use to you, don't thank only myself, but include in your gratitude all of those that have gone before, and hope they approve of the ways we use our skills and technology to improve our lives through music.

"For there is a music wherever there is a harmony, order or proportion; and thus far we may maintain the music of the spheres".

Sir Thomas Browne (1605–1682)

Bibliography

THE SECRETS OF STRADIVARI
  Simone F. Sacconi

Libreria del Convegno
Cremona 1979

LA MUSICA MEDIEVAL EN GALICIA
  Jose Lopez-Calo S. J.

*Fundacion ''Pedro Barrie de
la Maza'', Conde de Fenosa*
La Coruna 1982

EL PORTICO DE LA GLORIA
  Carlos Villanueva, Ed.

Universidad de Santiago
Santiago de Compostela 1988

SCIENCE AND MUSIC
  Sir James Jeans

Cambridge University Press
Cambridge 1961

THE ANATOMY OF WOOD
  K. Wilson and
  D.J.B. White

Stobart Davies
London 1986

THE COMPLETE MANUAL OF WOOD FINISHING
  Frederick Oughton

Stobart Davies Ltd.
London 1982

THE ILLUSTRATED HISTORY OF THE GUITAR
  Alexander Bellow

Colombo Publications
U.S.A. 1970

INSTRUMENTS OF THE MIDDLE AGES AND RENAISSANCE
  David Munroe

Oxford University Press
London 1976

DIE GITARRE UND IHR BAU
  Franz Jahnel

Verlag das Musikinstrument
Frankfurt am Main 1962

MAKE AND PLAY A LUTE
  Ronald Zachary Taylor

Argus Books Ltd.
London 1983

WOODWORK AIDS AND DEVICES
Robert Wearing

Unwin Hyman
London 1981

WORLD WOODS IN COLOUR
Wm. A. Lincoln

Stobart Davies
London 1986

Suppliers

Hand Tools

Clico (Sheffield) Tooling Ltd
Unit 7, Fell Road Industrial Estate, Sheffield S9 2AL

Mifer Tools U.K.
PO Box 85, Peterborough, Cambridgeshire, PE3 6FQ

Henry Taylor (Tools) Ltd
The Forge, Lowther Road, Sheffield, S6 2DR

Wood

Luthiers Supplies
The Hall, Horbeech Lane, Horam, East Sussex, TN21 0HR

Ronald Zachary Taylor
13, Churchfield Close, N. Harrow, Middlesex, HA2 6BD
(The author (above) will supply complete material packs for the individual instruments in this book)

Plans and Courses

Ronald Zachary Taylor
13, Churchfield Close, N. Harrow, Middlesex, HA2 6BD

West Dean College
West Dean, Nr. Chichester, West Sussex PO18 0QZ

Missenden Abbey
Great Missenden, Bucks HP16 0BD

Music and Strings

Early Music Shop
48 Great Marlborough Street, London W1V 2BN

(and author, see above)

Finishes

House of Harbru
101 Crostons Road, Elton, Bury, Lancs, BL8 1AL

John Myland Ltd.
80 Norwood High St., West Norwood, London SE27 9NW

Rustins Ltd
Waterloo Rd, Cricklewood, London NW2 7TX

Adhesives

Bison
Rowberry House, Copse Cross St, Ross-on-Wye, HR9 5PD

Craft Supplies Ltd
The Mill, Miller's Dale, Buxton, Derbyshire, SK17 8SN

(for Franklin's glue, see Luthiers Supplies, above)

SUPPLIERS IN THE U.S.A.

Franklin International
Corporate Center, 2020 Bruck St., Columbus, Ohio 43207

International Violin Co. Ltd.
4026 West Belvidere Avenue, Baltimore, Maryland 21215

Robert Meadows
2449 West Saugerties Road, Saugerties, NY 12477

Metropolitan Music Co. Ltd.
Box 1670 Mountain Rd., Vermont 05672

Musicmaker's Kits Inc.
423 S. Main, Stillwater, MN 55082

Luthiers Mercantile
PO Box 774, 412 Moore Lane, Healdsbury, CA 95448–0774

Woodcraft Corporation Inc.
313 Montvale Avenue, Woburn, Massachusetts 01801

SUPPLIERS IN CANADA

Unicorn Universal Woods Ltd
137 John St., Toronto, Ontario, M5V 2E4

A & M Wood Specialities
358 Eagle Street North, Cambridge, Ontario, N3H 4S6

SUPPLIERS IN GERMANY

Bruder Fuchs
Post Box 262, 8102 Mittenwald

Bernd Kurschner
Obere Waldstrasse 20, D-6204 Taunusstein-Wehen

ACKNOWLEDGEMENTS

Acknowledgements are due to Argus Books Ltd for their permission to use the illustrations of the Scraper Plane and Bridge Clamps, which appeared originally in "Make and Play a Lute" by Ronald Zachary Taylor.

Also to Ruth Brown and Theo Kanellos, who made, respectively, under the supervision of the author, the Gothic Harp and Flat-backed Mandolin which appear in this book. And to Mike Pattison who took the photographs of the instruments, including the front cover illustration.

INDEX